IN BATTLE &
CAPTIVITY
1916-1918

A BRITISH OFFICER'S MEMOIRS OF THE TRENCHES AND A GERMAN PRISON CAMP

BY
CAPTAIN GILBERT NOBBS

EDITED AND INTRODUCED BY
BOB CARRUTHERS

Pen & Sword
MILITARY

This edition published in 2014 by

Pen & Sword Military
An imprint of
Pen & Sword Books Ltd
47 Church Street
Barnsley
South Yorkshire
S70 2AS

This book was first published as 'On the Right of the British Line'
by Charles Scribner's Sons, New York, 1917.

ISBN: 9781783463121

A CIP catalogue record for this book is available from the British Library

Printed and bound in England
By CPI Group (UK) Ltd, Croydon, CR0 4YY

Pen & Sword Books Ltd incorporates the imprints of Pen & Sword Aviation, Pen & Sword
Family History, Pen & Sword Maritime, Pen & Sword Military, Pen & Sword Discovery, Pen
& Sword Politics, Pen & Sword Atlas, Pen & Sword Archaeology, Wharncliffe Local History,
Wharncliffe True Crime, Wharncliffe Transport, Pen & Sword Select, Pen & Sword Military
Classics, Leo Cooper, The Praetorian Press, Claymore Press, Remember When, Seaforth
Publishing and Frontline Publishing

For a complete list of Pen & Sword titles please contact

PEN & SWORD BOOKS LIMITED
47 Church Street, Barnsley, South Yorkshire, S70 2AS, England
E-mail: enquiries@pen-and-sword.co.uk
Website: www.pen-and-sword.co.uk

CONTENTS

INTRODUCTION

ORIGINALLY PUBLISHED IN 1917 as *On the Right of the British Line* this is the extraordinary autobiographical account of Henry Gilbert Nobbs an inspirational man of surprising energy and one of life's enduring monuments to the human spirit.

Henry Gilbert Nobbs was born in London in 1880, during the First World War, he served as a Captain in the London Rifle Brigade. In 1916 during the Somme Offensive, he led his company in an assault on the German trenches. In the close fighting he was shot through the head, and the bullet exited through his right eye, permanently blinding him. He lay in a shell-hole for two days, as the battle raged round him and woke up in a German hospital. After his wounds were treated he was sent to a POW camp. His next of kin had already been informed of his death and had received a telegram of condolences from Buckingham Palace, and it was a month before they learned the shocking truth. As a result of the severity of his injuries Captain Nobbs was repatriated to England where he composed this memoir of his experiences in the Great War.

He was sent to St. Dunstan's Home for blinded servicemen, which he was rather dreading, but to his surprise he found the atmosphere to be cheerful. He told the story in later years of how at one formal dinner there, he had thrown himself on the man seated next to him and began tickling him, crying out "Hullo, who do we have here then?" A voice replied "Derby" - it was Lord Derby, Secretary of State for War.

Nobbs emigrated to Australia with his wife and family in 1919, and threw himself into work for the firm of Holbrook's (Australasia) Ltd. He became the Managing Director of the company, and travelled widely on its behalf. Nobbs was granted the Freedom of the City of London, and was presented to the King and Prime Minister Ramsay MacDonald. Despite his enormous handicap he transformed Holbrook's into one of the largest employers in Australia.

In Manly, he was associated with Manly Amateur Swimming Club for many years, being vice-president in 1922, and President of the Club from 1924 onwards. He was also a vice-president and keen follower of the Manly Rugby Union club. He was also chairman of the NSW Blinded Soldiers' Association. He was awarded the OBE in the New Year's Day Honours of 1951 for his years of service.

His publications included *Rhymes and Reminiscences* (1922); and, of course the volume you hold here, *On the Right of the British Line*, which provides a vivid portrait of his wartime experiences; and *Blinded but Unbeaten* (1950), inspirational stories of blind achievement. Henry Gilbert Nobbs lived to the age of 90 and died in 1970, 54 years after his death had first been reported.

BOB CARRUTHERS

Captain Gilbert Nobbs.

PREFACE

THIS IS MY first book. It is also my last, but I have a record to make and a duty to perform. I was five weeks on the firing line; four weeks mourned as dead; and three months a prisoner of war.

I have attempted to make a true record of all that happened. The names alone are fictitious (all except that of Saniez), for those days were too full of stirring events which will long live in my memory to need the aid of fiction. If I have dwelt at some length upon my experience in Germany, it is with the hope that the information may be of interest to those who have relatives and friends still in the hands of the enemy and burn to know the truth.

I do not deplore the loss of my sight, for I can say in all sincerity that I was never happier in my life than I am today.

GILBERT NOBBS

BESIDES THE MAN WHO FIGHTS THERE IS
THE WOMAN WHO WAITS, AND IN HUMBLE
TRIBUTE TO HER SILENT HEROISM I
DEDICATE THIS BOOK

CHAPTER I
FOVANT

ORDERLY ROOM
OFF TO THE FRONT

"THE C.O. WANTS to see you."

"What for?" I asked.

"I don't know, but he is in the orderly room."

It was the adjutant who was speaking, and his manner led me to think there was something in the wind which he did not like to tell me. I left the mess, and a few moments later I was standing before the C.O.

"I have just received a telegram from the War Office; you are included in the next reinforcements for France."

"I am glad, sir."

"You've only forty-eight hours' notice. You are to report at Southampton at 4. P.M. the day after to-morrow."

"Very good, sir."

"Well, as your time is so short, you had better go home and get things ready. The adjutant will have your papers ready for you within half an hour."

"Very good, sir."

The C.O. stood up, and in his cordial military manner, which seemed to take you straight from the orderly room into the mess, held out his hand to bid me good-bye.

There is quite a difference between a C.O. in the orderly room and a C.O. in the mess. I mean those C. O.'s who are made of the right stuff, and our C.O. was certainly one of them.

In the orderly room his presence keeps you at arm's length and makes you feel that you want to keep clicking your heels and coming to the salute. You are conscious of the terrible crime you would commit if you permitted your body to relax from the position of attention; your conversational powers are restricted; you fancy you have a voice at the back of your head, saying:

"Don't argue, listen; digest, and get out."

It's a feeling which does not make the orderly room a very pleasant place to go to; yet you have an instinctive feeling of confidence.

The same C.O. in the mess, however, is a different man and creates quite a different atmosphere. In the orderly room he holds you from him; in the mess he pulls you to him. You have the feeling that you can sit in an armchair, with your feet on the coal-box, and talk to him round the corner of your newspaper, like the very ordinary human being he really is.

"Well, good-bye, and good luck." We shook hands, I came to the salute, and the next moment I found myself once more outside the orderly room door.

Have you ever experienced the feeling? Yes, thousands have, for the despatch of reinforcing officers to the front in this abrupt manner was taking place daily throughout the empire. You remember the feeling quite well; amazement at its suddenness; eagerness for the adventure; the prospect of the home parting; the sudden change in the daily routine; the mystery of the future — all swirling through your brain in a jumble of thoughts.

Then the hasty despatch of telegrams, the examination of time-tables, and the feverish packing of a kit which has grown to enormous proportions and hopelessly defies the regulations for weight.

An hour later and I had made a quick sale of my bicycle, distributed odds and ends of hut furniture which I should no longer need, and was sitting in a motor-car, outside the mess, grabbing at hands which were outstretched in farewell.

Those who lived in camp at Fovant can remember what an uninteresting, dreary place it seemed at the time, and how we cursed its monotony. Rows upon rows of uninteresting and uninviting looking huts; the large, barren square; the heart-breaking trudge to the station; the little village with the military policeman, who stood at the fork of the roads, and whose job seemed so easy, while ours seemed so hard;

and who always seemed so clean and cool, while we seemed so hot and dusty.

The city of Salisbury, our one ray of hope, but which was too far to walk to, and too expensive to ride to — all these things we used to look upon as sufferings which had to be put up with. But we can look upon the picture now, and there are few of us who can do so without a feeling of affection, for there was a spirit of comradeship there which links up the dreariness into pleasant recollections.

Now that I have been through the mill I can look back at that parting scene, and as the car whirls away and my brother officers walk back into the mess, I fancy I can hear the comment of those who had not yet been out and those who had:

"Lucky brute."

"Poor devil!"

CHAPTER II
THE SILENT HEROES
THE WOMAN WHO WAITS AND SUFFERS IN SILENCE

I WAS SOON comfortably settled in a first-class compartment and whirling towards Waterloo, with the worst ordeal of all still before me: the breaking of the news at home and the parting while the shock is still fresh.

Who are the true heroes of the war?

Our fighting men are cheered in the streets; every newspaper and magazine sings their praise; every shop-window reflects their needs; in theatre, pulpit, and workshop their praises are sung.

But are they the real heroes of the war?

Ask the fighting man himself. Speak to him of his wife or mother, and the expression on his face will answer your question.

There is no one to sing her praise, no one to paint the picture of her deeds; no one to tell of that lonely feeling when her hero departs and the door is closed behind him.

The fighting man looks upon his share of the war with a light heart. Events come too rapidly upon him to feel depressed. He does not feel the gnawing hunger of the lonely wait; the emptiness of the world when the parting is over; the empty chair at the table, and the rooms made cheerless by his absence.

There is no one to describe the terrors of the morning casualty list; the hourly expectation and frozen fear of the telegraph boy's "rat tat," bringing some dreadful news.

There are no crowds to cheer her; no flags or trumpets to rouse her enthusiasm and occupy her thoughts. No constant activity, thrilling excitement, desperate encounter.

Hers is a silent patriotism. She is the true hero of the war. And in hundreds of thousands of homes throughout the empire, her silent deeds, her wonderful fortitude, are making the womanhood of Britain a history which medals will not reward, nor scars display.

The fighting men know it, and when you cheer them, they know that there is still one at home who deserves your cheers, yet will not hear them; and who will seek no greater reward than the safe return of her own hero amid the applause which greets their homecoming.

Fighting men acknowledge it! And when your ears are no longer deafened by the cheers of others, take off your caps, fill your lungs, and cheer to the echo the real heroes of the war.

All honour to the woman who waits.

CHAPTER III
DEPARTURE FOR THE FRONT

WATERLOO STATION
LUNCHEON ARGUMENTS
THE BAGGAGE PROBLEM

WATERLOO STATION IN war time presents a picture of unending interest. Here it is that a thousand dramas are acted daily. It is one huge scene of bustle and excitement. The khaki of the soldier, the blue of the sailor; the mother, the wife, the sweetheart; the sad partings, the joyful greetings. The troops entraining, spick and span in their new war kit; the war-worn soldier home on leave, bespattered with the soil of France; troops from the near-by camps on week-end leave, tumbling out of the carriages with the spirits of schoolboys, or looking for standing-room in the overcrowded compartments on the last train back.

The scene is inspiring, depressing, historical.

Hear the noise and babble of the throng; the sobs and the cheers; the last look, the last handshake, the cheery greeting and the boyish laughter — whilst out in the street, London continues its unaltered ways, indifferent to the greatest war in the world's history reflected within a stone's throw, in Waterloo Station.

The Southampton train was rapidly filling, and I just managed to secure a seat and take a last look round. It needed a minute before the train was due to depart. Every window was filled with soldiers, and small groups were standing round each carriage door.

Porters were hurrying backward and forward, trying to find seats for late arrivals. Women were sobbing, men were talking earnestly. Presently the shrill whistle of the guard; hurried farewells, spontaneous cheers, and the slowly moving train gradually left the station, carrying its human freight to an unknown destiny.

I turned from the window and settled myself down in a corner. With me was Lieutenant Collins of our regiment, and Second Lieutenants Jones and Bailey of the London Regiment, while between us was a table laid for lunch.

"Well!" said Collins, packing his kit which had been dangling in a threatening manner from the rack, "that's one job over. I'm not sorry it's over, either. I wish we were coming back instead of going. I wouldn't mind getting a blighty wound in about a month's time. That would suit me down to the ground."

"Looking for trouble already," said Jones.

"You don't call that trouble, a nice little blighty wound, and then home."

"Don't be an idiot," I interrupted. "If every one felt the same way, who do you think is going to carry on the war?"

"Don't know. Never thought of it. But all the same a blighty wound in about a month's time will suit me down to the ground."

The conversation drivelled on in this way for a few miles, and finally turned into a heated discussion of the wine-list at the back of the menu.

Luncheon was served, and we were soon heavily engaged in a fierce attack on chicken and ham, intermingled with joke and arguments. The cause of the war and the prospect of its finish.

"Here's to a safe return," said Bailey, when his ginger ale had ceased to erupt its displeasure at being released from the bottle.

"And here's to an early blighty wound," said Collins.

"Hang it all," said Jones. "Can't you forget it?"

The conversation was bursting out afresh, and fortunately did not drift into politics or religion; and arguments easily turned to jokes, and jokes into a fresh onslaught on the chicken and ham.

There are some men who can argue best when armed with a knife and fork, and a good meal indisputably in their possession. There are others whose oratorical powers show greater promise when liquid refreshment is within easy grasp. In others yet again, the soothing influence of the twisted weed develops extraordinary powers. And before we arrived at Southampton town station the gift of each had full play.

We soon found ourselves scrambling amongst the heap of luggage which had been thrown in confusion on to the platform, and commenced an anxious search for our kits.

It is always the same at English railway stations, and our cousins from America and Canada scorn our system, or rather lack of system, for those who travel with baggage in England have always the possibility in front of them of a free fight to regain their possessions.

There seems to be only one thing to do if you are going to travel with a trunk, and that is either to paint it in rainbow colours, so that it will stand out in striking contrast to the mountainous heap of baggage thrown topsy-turvy out of the wagon on arrival at a terminus. Or, if not provided with this forethought of imagination, it is best to arrive at the starting station some hours ahead of time, and sit down on the platform and study the peculiarities of your trunk, its indentations and scratchings, and other characteristics, and committing all these details securely to your memory, so that when you arrive at the other end, and you jostle among the crowd gathered around the baggage-car, you can grab the collar of a porter and frantically shout: "There it is!" as it tumbles out of the wagon, to be finally submerged at the extreme bottom of the heap.

Unfortunately, all military kit bags are exactly the same. It is true you have your name painted on the outside, but so has everybody, and when fifty or sixty bags come tumbling out, they all look exactly alike.

That is how it was at Southampton town station, but we were all in good spirits, thanks to the wine-list before mentioned; and as all the owners of the kit bags were carrying an uncomfortable amount of ordnance stores on their backs, the heap of luggage soon became submerged beneath a still greater heap of energetic and perspiring humanity, until the scene looked net unlike a very much disturbed ant-hill.

But I am exaggerating. Yet, the exaggeration of my words, written in a calm moment of thought is far less vociferous than the exaggerated words used at the time during the frantic endeavour to seek one's solitary kit bag, and extricate it in such a scramble.

But at last the four of us, bent double by our packs, and freely perspiring in the heat of an August day, could be seen rolling, pushing, kicking, and dragging our worldly belongings off the platform towards the station entrance, to seek the hospitality of an ancient hack. And then we drove away, our kit and our equipment stacked high around us at precarious angles, and completely submerging the occupants, to the delight of the people who stood and watched us in open-mouthed amazement.

CHAPTER IV
CROSSING THE CHANNEL

THE DOCK PORTER
A WHIFF OF BOND STREET

A RRIVING AT THE dock we reported to the embarkation officer, and were given a pass to leave the dock, but bearing the strict injunction that we must embark at 6 P.M..

When you cross to France for the first time you are so nervous about missing the boat and running the risk of a court-martial, or some other such dreadful suggestion, that you hardly dare to leave the dock gates, and you are certainly waiting at the gang-plank a full fifteen minutes before the appointed time.

But those who are no longer novices to the mysterious calculation of those who regulate our army traffic, would, on receiving such instruction, immediately repair to the best hotel, there to regale themselves in a glorified afternoon tea, and afterwards seat themselves in the front row at the local Empire; subsequently rolling up at the ship's side shortly after 9 o'clock, to find that the troop-ship is not due to sail for another hour at least.

Having enjoyed all the pleasure of such disregard to orders, and arriving in due course at the ship's side, I searched around for my baggage and for means of getting it on board. I had not far to look, for there were a number of soldiers standing about, whose evident duty it was to do the necessary fatigue work.

I call them soldiers because they were dressed in khaki; but the King's uniform could not disguise the fact that they were the old-time dock porters. There is something about the earnest, anxious look of the dock porter, as he tenders you his services, which even the martial cut of a military uniform cannot hide. His adopted profession in peace, inscribed so deeply in his face and bearing, cannot be hidden so easily by the curtain of war.

A lance corporal approached me, and, assuring me that nothing would go astray that was left in his charge, slung my kit over his shoulder with professional skill and followed me up the gangplank, placing my belongings carefully down in what may once have been the cabin of the ship. He crossed his legs, leaned heavily with one arm on my baggage, and tipping his cap on the back of his head to enable me to see the exact amount of perspiration upon his forehead, and breathing heavily, so that I might form an exact estimate of the fatigue he had undergone, he waited in hopeful expectancy.

I gave him a tip.

It is against all regulations to tip a soldier; but it seemed such a natural thing to do, for his khaki uniform could not hide the habit of years.

He did not salute, but touched his cap. I smiled to myself as I watched him depart. He was a soldier now; but the uniform could not disguise the fact that he was still a dock porter.

We had a splendid crossing, and I shall not readily forget the romantic atmosphere of that night. The sea was calm, and a full moon cast a silvery, shimmering pathway across the water.

All lights on board the troop-ship were extinguished, and with black smoke belching from the funnels, and the vibrations of the engines trembling through the ship, we made our dash across the Channel.

Who but those whose duty it is to perform the arduous task of protecting our troop-ships can understand and appreciate what it means to live the life of the sailor on those comfortless -looking destroyers.

Night after night, week after week, throughout the years, tearing frantically up and down, seeking a hidden foe; daring the treacherous mines; safeguarding their trust with apparent disregard for their own safety.

The men who perform such duties are hidden heroes; and the safe transportation of our fighting millions across the seas is a silent tribute of their bravery.

This work goes on, and will go on until the end of the war, and the men who perform this great task do so with the knowledge that only failure can bring their names before the public.

I met many old friends on board, and several new ones. But one man in particular attracted my attention, for his appearance seemed so strangely out of place with the surroundings.

Standing near the companionway, and looking upon the scene with a bored expression, was a young man in the thirties, in a brand-new uniform, with a single star on his shoulder-strap, which proclaimed him to the world as a second lieutenant.

He was rather tubby in appearance, with a round, chubby face, which was screwed up in a frantic effort to retain within its grasp a monocle, through which he viewed his fellow beings in mute astonishment; and what is more, he wore new kid gloves. It was Septimus D'Arcy, dressed in immaculate neatness, radiating the atmosphere of Bond Street; indifferent to everybody, yet with a horrified look of discomfort at finding himself in such unusual surroundings.

I had hardly turned from the strange scene when Collins caught hold of my arm.

"Come over here; I want to introduce you to a friend of mine, who, I believe, is coming out to be attached to us," he said.

We walked along the deck, and, to my embarrassment, a few moments later I found myself shaking the limp paw of Septimus D'Arcy, glove and all.

I am not quite sure that Septimus, on my introduction, did anything more than open his mouth, while I raised and lowered his right forearm. Septimus would have spoken, I quite sure, as the movement of his mouth indicated that such was his intention; although the expression, or rather lack of expression, on his face, bore no proof that his remarks, if uttered, would be very interesting. In fact, Septimus needed encouragement.

"We are having a very pleasant crossing," I ventured.

"Ye-s," he drawled, "but a demned overcrowded one — what?"

"I suppose so, but troop-ships are always overcrowded."

"I say, though, where does one sleep?"

I rather suspected that what Septimus really wanted to know was whether there was such a thing to be had as a private cabin, where he could disrobe his tubby figure in seclusion.

"There seems to be two places to sleep," I replied; "either in the boiler-room or on deck."

"On deck! Rather uncomfortable — what?"

"Well not nearly so uncomfortable as it may be later. I am just going down to get my kit and lay it out on deck," I said. "Hadn't you better get yours, too?"

I went down below, leaving Septimus with his mouth still open, and his round nose wrinkled up with an expression of discomfort. But he made no move to accept my invitation.

I unrolled my kit on the deck by the side of a long row of officers who were already comfortably settled for the night. On either side of each officer were his war kit and a life-belt.

I got into my sleeping-bag, and not feeling very sleepy, I lit a cigarette and looked upon my surroundings.

The scene was a very inspiring one, and I could not help dreaming of the future. What had destiny in store for us? Who would return in glory? And who would be called upon to pay the great price — to come back bleeding and disabled, dependent for future existence upon the benevolence of a nation's gratitude?

The ship sped onward, carrying its human freight. Greater and greater grew the distance from loved ones left behind. Nearer and nearer we sped towards the unknown future.

How many of those lying around, silent companions of their thoughts, were thinking the same as I?

What was the future? Horror, anxiety, success, failure, mutilation, death; which was it to be? And what a change this was to the times we had had in the past.

We were all civilian soldiers: lawyers, merchants, bankers, and tradesmen. Fighting was not our profession nor desire.

Whose power was it to transform these lives so ruthlessly from the habits of peace to become instruments of war? Whose was the hand which plucked us from homes and families, to hurl us into the caldron of hell? Was it the ambition of a nation, guided by the despotic direction of a tyrant?

We knew it and believed it. We could not remain idle to see our homes and families suffering the destruction and barbarities inflicted on Belgium. The fire of hell blazed by the petrol of German fury must not be wafted in the direction of our beloved country.

The call had been answered, and these silent forms of England's sons were speeding through the night in the direction of danger, at the bidding of a nation in peril.

My cigarette was finished, and I was becoming sleepy. I turned over to settle myself comfortably, and turning my eyes in the direction of the companionway, I saw the tubby figure of an officer standing near the rail, immaculately dressed, and in strange contrast to his surroundings.

It was Septimus D'Arcy, immaculate and indifferent. Septimus was at war; but Septimus was still in Bond Street.

CHAPTER V
GOING UP THE LINE

PERFIDIOUS GANG-PLANKS
D'ARCY STRANDED
GUIDES WHO CANNOT GUIDE
A HEATED ARGUMENT

NEXT MORNING WE were disturbed early, and rolled up our kits ready for disembarkation.

About 7 A.M. we pulled alongside the wharf, and a light-hearted, jostling crowd struggled for the gang-plank.

I have not yet been able to find out why gangplanks are made so narrow, so that only one person at a time dare undertake the passage.

Chaos seemed to prevail. The deck suddenly became a struggling mass of humanity, struggling, tugging, and dragging at valises and kit bags.

Officers were manfully shouldering their "marching order," and struggling with their valises, hoping that their turn would come to find a footing on the gang-plank.

The gang-plank was long and narrow, bending and squeaking under its burden. There were two gang-planks: one to go down and one to come up.

But we were not sailors, and did not know the system; the inevitable result being that those going up met those coming down, until they became an unwieldy medley of men, baggage, protests, and apologies.

Gang-planks at the best of times appear structures of absurdity. They either appear to be placed at an angle so dangerous that the only safe way of getting ashore appears to be to sit down and slide. At other times the gang-plank has an unhappy knack of sagging in a precarious manner as you approach the middle, while a couple of sailors hold desperately on to the end to prevent its slipping off the dock.

Here we reported to the landing officer, who was making frantic endeavours to create order from chaos.

In circumstances of this kind the best thing to do with the landing officer is to keep clear of him. So we seized the only hack available and drove to one of the leading hotels, which had the reputation of being popular.

I am not quite sure if these conveyances are called hacks, but the name seems very appropriate; for carriage seems too dignified a term for such dilapidated vehicles.

We were, however, too glad to get away as rapidly as possible from the dusty deck, and it was already getting very hot.

Turning into one of the side streets, we beheld the immortal Septimus, looking like one who is hopelessly lost in the middle of the Sahara Desert.

Now Septimus was not a born soldier, and he had made no attempt to carry his equipment on his back; neither would it seem right for Septimus to carry any greater burden on his podgy form than his well-polished Sam Brown. So his equipment lay on the pavement beside him. He had evidently dragged it some little distance, and looked upon it as a beastly nuisance, and was standing there vainly hoping that a taxi would come to his rescue and help him carry the beastly thing away.

We gave Septimus a lift, as he evidently needed looking after.

Arriving at the hotel, we all tumbled into the dining-room for breakfast, all except Septimus D'Arcy, who made straight for the nearest bar, and was last heard of that day tapping a coin vigorously on the counter, and with the perspiration standing in beads on his nose, frantically screeching for a whisky and soda.

Two days later I received a slip of paper which warned me that I was to proceed up the line that evening.

I was a senior officer, and would have charge of all the troops departing that evening. If you have never had that job, take my tip and avoid it; for of all the thankless tasks the poor devil who suddenly finds himself O. C. train, has the most difficult one of all.

I reported to the camp adjutant, an awfully decent sort of chap, and as a farewell gift he placed in my hands a pile of documents and several sheets of printed instructions.

"There you are, old chap, you will find everything there."

"Why, what is all this about?" said I, holding on to the mysterious bundle of papers which he thrust into my hands.

"That is a complete record, in duplicate, of all the troops in your charge. When you get to the station hand those papers over to the R. T. O."

"How many men have I charge of?"

"Rather a big crowd going tonight — 38 officers and 1,140 other ranks."

"What regiments do they belong to?"

"Well, I think you have got men who belong to nearly every regiment serving in France. There are reinforcement draughts going to various units, and numerous men returning from leave. You've got English, Scotch, Canadians, and Australians. You've got cavalrymen, artillerymen, engineers, and infantrymen. Believe me, you've got your hands full to-night.

"You will find a guide at the head of the column who knows the way to the station. It's a good five miles from here."

When I got outside I found the column nearly a quarter of a mile long, formed up ready to march off.

I gave the order to move to all those within reach of my voice, and trusted to the remainder to follow on.

It was quite dark as the long column moved slowly down the long boulevards. I had not the faintest notion where the station was. Wherever I went that long, unwieldy column would slowly follow me, and trust blindly to my direction. I pinned my faith to the guide, and on we went.

Before we had got half-way it became evident that the guide had a very remote idea which was the direction to take; and he began to make anxious inquiries of passers-by as to the right way.

I was beginning to feel anxious and lose patience.

"What are you fussing about for? Are you taking us the right way?" I demanded.

"I think so, sir. I don't know."

"You don't know! But you are the guide, aren't you?"

"Yes, sir. But I've never been to the station before."

"But you are supposed to be the guide. Do you mean to tell me that you are not sure of the way?"

"Not quite, sir. But I am doing my best."

"Well, you are a fine sort of guide! Who detailed you?"

"The adjutant, sir."

"Well, did he know you had never been down to the station before?"

"He never asked me, sir. I was not doing any other duty, so he detailed me to act as your guide."

What staff work! But it served me right; and we muddled along, and finally, to my great relief, we entered the station yard.

I walked into the R. T. O.'s office and laid my pile of papers on his desk.

The railway transport officer is an individual who is prominent in the memory of all those who have passed up the line; and many of us have reason to remember at least one of them with indignation.

There are two kinds of R. T. O.'s, and you have met them both.

There is the one who has earned his job at the front by hard work. He has been through the thick of the fighting, and after months in the trenches has been sent back to act as R. T. O. at the rail-head or the base, to give him a well-earned rest beyond the sound of the guns. We have no unpleasant memories of him. He is a man; he is human; he treats you as a comrade; he is helpful and considerate. And you can spot such men in a moment.

But R. T. O. No. 2 carries no sign of war on his features. He has never heard the sound of guns, and never intends to, if he can help it.

Look back upon the time when you left the base, and you find him prominent in your memory. When you are huddled up in your dugout, how you wish he could be transferred to you for a tour of duty in the trenches.

What a delight it would be to send him in his immaculate uniform; his highly polished leggings and boots, along the muddy communication trenches. You know what the feeling is, for oftentimes you have said to yourself in those lonely night-watches: "How I wish I had him here!"

It is 2 o'clock in the morning; the rain is coming down in torrents; danger lurks in every fire-bay; the loneliness and the weirdness give you the creeps.

How you wish you could wake him up by digging him in the ribs, and telling him that it is time to go on his tour of duty up and down those clay-sodden trenches at the hour of the night when his courage (if he ever had any) would be at its lowest.

What a delight it would be if we only had him with us when we take over our trenches, to show him that foul-smelling, rat-ridden dugout, and tell him to curl himself up to sleep there.

How sweet would be the joy to see him in his pale-coloured breeches, huddled up in a saphead, trying to get a little comfort on a cold, raw December morning, from a drop of tea in a tin mug, well smudged with the wet clay of numerous fingers.

CHAPTER VI
RATIONS

I LEARN TO HATE FOOD
MATHEMATICAL PROBLEMS

W E ARRIVED AT Rouen at 7.30 the following morning. I had to report to the R. T. O. by 9.30, and in the meantime 3,534 rations had to be cut up and distributed on the station platform among 1,178 officers and men.

Have you ever had such a problem as that? If not, then avoid it, if it ever comes your way.

The train was about twice the length of the platform, so on arrival it was broken in half, and the rear half shunted on to another line.

The rations were contained in two trucks, attached to the rear half of the train, so the contents had to be carried by hand across several sets of rails, to the end of the platform.

I had a fatigue party of 60 men at work, and presently a huge quantity of provisions began to pile up. There were chests of tea, cases of biscuits, cases of jam, cases of bully beef, sugar, and bacon sufficient to fill the warehouse of a wholesale provision merchant.

Three days' rations for 1,178 officers and men, in bulk; and 1,178 officers and men began to gather around the stack, in hungry expectancy of breakfast.

Now to issue rations to a battalion straight from bulk is quite difficult enough, but to issue rations from bulk to units of various strengths, belonging to over fifty regiments is enough to drive any one crazy.

Each man was entitled to two and one-fourth ounces of tea, one-fourth ounce of mustard, two and one-fourth pounds of biscuits, three-fourths pound of cheese, twelve ounces of bacon, one tin of bully beef, nine ounces of jam.

Each unit had to be dealt with separately, so that each unit presented a mathematical problem of the most perplexing kind. Each unit sent up its fatigue party to draw rations, whilst I and several officers who had volunteered to assist me made a bold attempt at distribution.

"Come along, first man, what's your regiment?"

"Manchester, sir; 59 men."

I looked through my volume of papers to check his figures.

"Quite right! Fifty-nine men."

Fifty-nine men meant fifty-nine times two and one-fourth ounces of tea, one-fourth ounce of mustard, two and one-fourth pounds of biscuits, three-fourths pound of cheese, twelve ounces of bacon, one tin of bully beef, and nine ounces of jam. My brain whirls when I think of those problems.

The next unit consisted of 9 men; the next of 1; then came a long list of 2's, 5's, and 7's, and so on; and in each case the mathematical problem had to be worked out; and when the figuring was finished, the stuff had to be cut up.

Seventy-nine pounds of cheese for the Manchester; does any one know what seventy-nine pounds of cheese looks like? No one did; we had never seen so much cheese before in our lives.

"Give him a whole cheese and chance it. And now tea; the Manchesters want one hundred and thirty-two and three-fourths ounces of tea. Give him about three handfuls and chance it."

The next party consisted of 2 men.

"Six ounces of jam for the 19 Canadians; how much is that?"

"Nearly half a pot."

"What are you going to put it in?"

"Got nothing."

"Can't have any, then?"

"Come on, next man."

When I saw the last of that stack of food it was 11.30. We were hungry and tired, and we made our way to the nearest hotel, fervently hoping that we might never see food in bulk again.

CHAPTER VII
ST. AMAND

I REPORT AT HEADQUARTERS
THE PROBLEM OF VENTILATION

WE MADE OUR way back to the station and secured a very luxurious compartment; and to my intense relief on this occasion I found there was an officer senior to me present, who succeeded to the duties of O. C. train.

The duties of O. C. train are a new sensation to most officers; and it is particularly difficult to know just what to do, and how to do it, when you have an unorganised body of men made up of sundries from every part of the British army.

Our new O. C. train evidently felt the difficulties of his position, and came to me for assistance.

"Excuse me," he said, "but were you in charge of the train last night?"

"Yes, sir. I'm sorry to say I was."

"Well, what does one have to do?"

"Nothing."

"Well, but how does one keep order?"

"One doesn't keep order. But they've given me a pile of printed instructions, and I don't see how they can possibly be carried out. How can I keep order in a train half a mile long with men I know nothing about?"

He was getting worried. I knew the feeling.

"Do you want a tip," I said.

"Yes, if you can give me one."

"Well, just walk along the train until you find a very comfortable compartment marked, 'O. C. train.' Get inside, lock the door, pull down the blinds and go to sleep."

"Thanks, awfully. I think I'll take that tip."

"By the way," I shouted after him, "what is our destination?"

"Haven't the faintest idea."

"Does anybody know?"

"I don't think so."

"Thanks, awfully."

The train journey was uneventful, save for alternatively eating and sleeping, and two days later I reported at battalion headquarters.

The battalion was in rest billets at St. Amand; and I was posted as second in command to B Company.

The officers of B Company were just about to begin their midday meal when I put in an appearance at the company mess.

Captain George commanded the company. He was a splendid type of the righting man of the present day — young, active, and clear-cut, boyish, yet serious. Captain George was made of the right stuff, and we became chums on the spot.

The other officers of the company were Second Lieutenant Farman, who had just received his commission in the field, Second Lieutenant Chislehirst, and Second Lieutenant Day.

They were all splendid fellows, the type you meet and take to at once; all as keen as ginger when there is serious work to be done; and when work is over are as light-hearted as schoolboys.

The mess consisted of a dilapidated kitchen, with a stone floor, and ventilated by the simple method of broken windows and a door removed from the hinges.

In those northern farmhouses of France it is purely a matter of opinion as to whether ventilation is really an advantage; for from the yard in front of the house the odour from the refuse and manure of the farm, piled up in a heap outside your window, becomes very acute when the wind is in the wrong direction, as it usually is.

CHAPTER VIII
EARLY IMPRESSIONS

BILLETS
A STARTLING INCIDENT
REST CAMP

I SHALL NEVER forget the day I made my first inspection of billets. While walking through the village street I noticed a structure which appeared to be inviting some stray breath of wind to cause it to surrender its last resistance by collapsing into a heap of rubbish.

Many years ago, in days of prosperity, it had served the purpose of a covering for cattle, for I believe cattle are not very particular in northern France.

It is quite within reason to suppose that, with a view of misleading his cattle into a false sense of security, the farmer may have called it a barn. It had never been an expensive structure, nor did it give any evidence of having ever laid claim to architectural beauty.

But its simplicity of construction was a marvel of ingenuity. Yes, it was a barn, but who but a genius of modern arts would have thought it possible to build even a barn by the simple but equally economical method of erecting a number of props and simply sticking mud between?

But the stability of the barn was, as might reasonably be supposed, subject to "wind and weather permitting," and was now sorrowfully deploring its advancing years, and anxiously waiting an early opportunity to rest its weary limbs in a well-earned rest in a shapeless heap on the ground that gave it birth.

How very strange! Out of the numerous holes in the wall I saw familiar faces, while inside a score of men were laughing and joking, playing cards or lounging about in loose attire, as though they were enjoying the freedom and comfort of a West End club.

"But what are you men doing here?" I asked.

"This is our billet, sir," answered a lance corporal.

"Your billet? Do you mean you sleep here?"

"Yes, sir, this was allotted to half my platoon."

"Comfortable?"

"Yes, sir. Quite a treat after the trenches."

"A bit draughty, isn't it?"

"Yes, sir; but, like everything else, we have to get used to it."

"But can't you find a better place than this, and with more room? You seem to be almost on top of each other."

"There is no other place available. The men are quite satisfied, sir."

I turned away thoughtfully. What magnificent chaps! And yet, when they were in comfortable billets at Haywards Heath, or in well-built huts at Fovant, they were far more particular; when they were recruits and spent their first night in the army, they looked with dismay at the prospect of sleeping on a clean straw mattress in a well-built modern English house.

War makes men, and hardships breed content!

I will pass over our life in the trenches in this part of the line, but an incident worth recording occurred while we were marching back after five days amongst the rats and mud of the trenches facing Gommecourt Wood.

It is interesting, by the way, to watch the men leaving the trenches for their rest billets, for, in addition to their packs, they carry many an additional article of private belongings to add to their comfort during these tedious days of duty, and they emerge with all kinds of curious packages and extra articles of clothing strapped or tied to their equipment. They were covered with mud and clay before they left the front-line trenches, but the long journey along endless communication trenches on their way out, gathered up an additional covering of clay and mud through their bulky attire, until they resembled a curious assembly of moving debris.

But the incident I have referred to occurred just as we were approaching a village.

An observation balloon was being drawn down, but when within a hundred feet of the ground suddenly broke away and began to rise rapidly and drift towards the German lines.

I halted the men, and we watched in breathless suspense the tragedy which was about to take place before our eyes. There was some one in the basket of the balloon.

It rose higher and higher. Nothing could save it! Presently the occupant was seen to lean over the side and throw out a quantity of books and papers.

Still upward it went, and seemed to reach a great height before the next sensation caused us to thrill with amazement.

Something dropped like a stone from the basket and then, with a sudden check, a parachute opened, and a man was seen dangling from it. When he dropped, the balloon must have been many thousand feet in the air, and both balloon and parachute continued to drift towards the German lines.

Then a flight of four or five British aeroplanes went up and soared around the balloon, evidently bent on its destruction.

As we watched we saw a flash and a puff of smoke! A bomb had struck the balloon, but seemed to have no effect.

The aeroplanes withdrew, and a minute later we heard the boom of the anti-aircraft guns.

The second shot was a dead hit, for we saw a flash of fire clean through the centre, a volume of blue smoke, and then it buckled in the middle. The flame spread, and the blue smoke increased in volume until the balloon resembled a curious shapeless mass, twisting and turning and shrinking as it quivered and fell to earth; meantime, anxious eyes were also turned to the parachute, which by this time had approached to within a few hundred feet or so of the earth.

Both armies must have watched the spectacle in silent wonder, for no shot was fired at the falling figure from the German lines.

It was difficult to tell from where we were just where it might fall. It seemed to me from where I stood that the odds were in favour of it reaching the ground in No Man's Land.

As it neared the earth it began to sway to and fro, in ever-increasing violence, and finally disappeared from view behind a clump of trees. So far as I could observe, it did not seem in any way possible for the parachute to have delivered its human freight safely to the earth.

Next day we began a three days' march to a village some thirty-eight miles back of the line.

We were to be rested and fattened for the Somme.

The mention of rest camps to men at the front generally raises a smile, for if there is one thing more noticeable than anything else during a rest period, it is the hard work which has to be done.

The long days of training, the unlimited fatigue work, and the never-ending cleaning of tattered uniforms and trench-soiled boots are equalled only by the fastidiousness of an Aldershot parade.

CHAPTER IX

DEPARTURE FOR THE SOMME

CORBIE
HAPPY VALLEY
PASSING THROUGH THE GUNS

O N SUNDAY, SEPTEMBER 2, our so-called rest came to an abrupt finish, and we entrained for an unknown destination. Destinations are always a mystery until the train pulls up with a jerk, and peremptory orders are given to get out.

The difference in travelling as a civilian and travelling as a soldier is that in the former case you choose your time of departure or arrival at a convenient hour; while in the latter case the most unearthly hour is selected for you.

We arrived at Corbie at 2 A.M. Not that we knew it was Corbie at the time, or cared; and even if we had known, we should have been little the wiser. Still, I will say this about Corbie, that it is pronounced in the way it is spelled, and that relieves one of a sense of uneasiness. For, as a general rule, no matter how you pronounce the names of a French town, you will find some one with an air of superior knowledge, or gifted with a special twist of the tongue, who will find a new pronunciation.

However, we detrained onto the line. The night was as black as pitch. Sleepy soldiers, struggling with their equipment, dropped out of the carriages; and after a great deal of shouting we got into some kind of formation, and the long column slowly moved off into the night.

I dropped into position in the rear of the column, feeling very tired, and wondering where I should find a place to sleep. The long column wended its way through narrow streets and along cobbled roads, and gradually seemed to melt into mysterious doorways under the guiding influence of quartermaster sergeants.

This process went on until I suddenly realised that the whole column had disappeared, and I was left alone in the streets of Corbie at 3 A.M. in a steady downpour of rain, without the faintest notion of where I was, or where my billet was. I walked a little farther down the street, and being very tired, wet, and sleepy, had almost decided to lie in the street until the morning, when I tumbled across Farman, Chislehirst, and Day following the faithful quartermaster-sergeant to an unknown billet.

The billet consisted of a bathroom in one of the outbuildings of a large estate. The door of the bathroom had been locked, and the water had been turned off. However, we scrambled through the window. The floor was hard, but we had a roof above our heads, and we were all soon snoring on the floor, fast asleep.

Next morning I took a walk around the estate and found myself in a lovely orchard. It was deserted. An abundance of most delicious fruit met my gaze wherever I went. I wandered up and down, picking the apples and the pears, biting the fruit and throwing it away. I felt like a bad boy in an orchard; but the orchard was deserted and the fruit was going to waste; so if I was looting, I consoled myself with the thought that I was preventing waste.

It was about 1.30 in the afternoon, and I had just settled myself down in a comfortable seat under an apple-tree, and had pulled a Sunday newspaper out of my pocket; it was a hot September day, and I was feeling lazy.

I was bound for the Somme. There was a mysterious air about the place that seemed unnatural. These beautiful gardens were deserted, but the sound of the guns could be heard in the distance.

I had settled myself comfortably, trying to imagine with the aid of the Sunday paper and a cigar that I was really sitting in my own gardens, when I noticed a man filling his water-bottle.

"What are you filling your water-bottle for?" I asked.

"We have got orders to parade at 2 o'clock, to move off."

"Good Lord! Who told you that?"

"Captain Wilkie, sir. The orders have just come down."

I never had such a scramble in my life. With an appetite over satisfied with apples; my kit spread all over the floor; my company half a mile away in all sorts of holes and corners — to move out of the village in twenty minutes.

It's the same old thing in the army; you say to yourself it can't be done; but it is done. And at five minutes past two the whole brigade was moving out of Corbie, and was once more facing towards the Somme.

Our destination was in Death Valley; but before going into the line we rested a few days in Happy Valley. Happy Valley and Death Valley — there is a touch of sarcasm about the names, but they are, nevertheless, very appropriate.

Happy Valley is a peaceful spot where we would sit contentedly in the afternoon purring at our pipes, listening to the sound of the guns; watching the shrapnel bursting in the air some two or three miles away, and thanking our lucky stars that we were watching it from a distance. But we were resting. It was a lull before the storm, and we were soon to march towards the storm.

Death Valley was three miles away, and tomorrow the storm would break upon us! We were thinking; men everywhere were writing. Why were they biting their pencils and thinking so hard? The padre was a busy man. Everything was so quiet and mysterious: there was no joking, no laughing, men were thoughtful and pulled hard at their pipes. To-morrow the storm would break! To-morrow! And what after?

The following afternoon, after struggling across a sea of shell-holes, we arrived at Death Valley and halted by Trones Wood. Here hundreds of our guns of all sizes were massed, wheel to wheel, and row upon row; and every gun was being worked as hard as possible.

A bombardment was taking place. And in the midst of all these guns we were halted for two hours until our trenches could be located. The sight was wonderful. It was impressive. The might of Britain was massed and belching forth its concentrated fury.

As darkness came on the roar of the guns was accentuated by the flash of the discharge. We did not speak, for speaking was out of the question; the noise was too terrific; and we lay on the ground silenced by wonder and bewilderment.

What was happening over yonder where those shells were dropping? What was that droning, whistling noise far overhead? They were the big guns: the 15-inch, five miles back; 16-pounders, 4.9-inch, 6-inch, 9-inch, 12-inch, and 15-inch. Guns here, guns there, guns everywhere; all belching and flashing; all concentrating in a stupendous effort to pound some part of the German line into confusion.

Ammunitions workers in England, and those who should be munition workers, come right over here; creep with us along the edge of Trones Wood, and watch this amazing sight. You miners, you tramway men, you boiler-makers! You, who would throw down your tools and strike, look upon this sight!

This is the voice of England. This is the stupendous effort which is protecting you. On your right, that dark, creepy, silent place, is Trones Wood. Look across to your left, those sticks showing on the sky-line, across the valley. In those woods, churned up in the soil, lie the rotting bodies of your comrades, your brothers, your sons. They have sacrificed all; they have suffered untold deaths.

The contrast between that thundering voice of England and the silent mystery of those woods causes a shudder. Bring out those strikers and let them get a glimpse of this and realise their danger, and the horrors which will come upon them, their wives, their children, their homes, if those guns fail.

What is their quarrel to this? Shall we stop those guns for a penny an hour? Shall we leave unprotected those desperate men across the valley, who are hanging on tooth and nail to those last trenches gained? Shall we do these things for a penny an hour? Shall we do these things so that we can stand up for these so-called rights in England?

No! Our mines must be worked; our boilers must be made; and our munition machinery must be run to its utmost capacity, or we are traitors to those guns and our fighting men; our brothers, our own sons, who are depending upon the might of England for victory and their lives.

Throw down your tools, slacken your machinery, and High Wood and Trones Wood will become blacker still with the mutilated bodies of a thousand men. A penny an hour! You, who are being coddled under the protection of these guns, what is your quarrel to this?

If those desperate fellows on the other side of the hill were to leave their tasks, they would be called traitors. Yet, when men in England, whom these fighters are dependent upon, and whose work is just as necessary for the success of the war, throw down their tools, they are only called strikers.

The crime is the same; the punishment should be the same.

CHAPTER X
ARRIVAL ON THE SOMME

FEEDING THE GUNS
SEPTIMUS D'ARCY ARRIVES
A CURIOUS KIT

L ATE THAT EVENING orders came to move into the trenches on the far slope of the Valley of Death. Trenches here, trenches there, trenches everywhere, while we groped around without knowing where the trenches led to, or the position of the German lines.

We spent an anxious night, the uncertainty of our position and mystery of those massed guns, thundering their wrath into the darkness of the night, caused a tension which defied any desire to sleep.

What was the meaning of it all? What was happening over yonder, where the iron of England's anger was falling, bursting, tearing, killing? What was happening over there? Would we receive a similar reply? The signs were significant: we were at last on the Somme; we were in for it with a vengeance.

The next morning broke bright and fair, and found us still awake with eyes peering anxiously through the rising mist. We were evidently not in the front line, but were there on the Somme; and that sea of shell-holes which everywhere surrounded us told its own story of what had been, and what was yet to be.

At about 11 o'clock all eyes were turned towards High Wood, on the crest of the hill to the left. A burst of shells from the enemy's guns told that a target had been found. We watched, and presently we could faintly see a column slowly moving along the road through the wood.

Three ammunition wagons moved slowly towards our guns. Crash! A 5.9 fell in front of the leading horses; a cloud of dense, black smoke arose and blotted the picture from view. The smoke cleared, and the little column was still moving slowly forward, undisturbed and indifferent.

Crash! Crash! Two more shells burst by the side of the second wagon; the smoke cleared; the horses were startled and giving trouble, but once again the defiant little column moved slowly forward, indifferent and undismayed.

We continued to watch the plucky little column, now obscured by the black smoke of the bursting shells, then again emerging from the smoke, heedless of danger.

Those men were human. How could they stand it with such calm and determined indifference? The answer was the guns: the guns must be fed; and British grit and discipline were unconquerable. The army is wonderful.

At this moment I received a message calling me to headquarters, and I at once went to find my C.O.

"Well, had a good rest?" he asked.

"Not much, sir."

"Stuff and nonsense; get your map out."

I spread my map out on my knees and took a note-book out of my pocket.

The CO. pointed on the map with his pencil:

"We are here; the Regiment — is there."

"Front line, sir?"

"Right bang up in the front line."

"What are the trenches like, sir?"

"No time to dig trenches; they're hanging on to a few shell-holes, though they may have connected them up by now. See, there's Combles, and that's Leuze Wood. We shall be on the extreme right of the British army. B Company will be on the right; C Company in the centre, and A Company on the left with D Company in support. Headquarters will be close by Falfemont Farm."

"Very good, sir."

"You won't find any farm left; been blown to dust. Men are to go in battle order; packs are to be parked just outside here, by companies. No. 5 platoon will move off at 7 P.M., the remainder following in succession at fifty yards' interval."

I understood, and turned to go.

"By the way, I am not sure whether the Germans are in that trench or the — Battalion, London Regiment. Anyhow, that's where we've got to be to-night."

Half an hour later and the men were laying out their packs in long rows, by companies. Strange sight, all these packs laid out in neat rows. The reason did not need explaining. There was work at the other end of that Valley of Death; there lay the pit of the Great Adventure. Perhaps tonight we should look into it; but how many would come back to claim their packs.

We are in the soup with a vengeance! Well, who cares?

Early that afternoon I went to my dugout, and was just trying to get a little rest, when I was disturbed by a voice outside, which sounded strangely familiar.

"Sergeant, excuse me, but is this the beastly hole where B Company is to be found?"

"Yes, sir, this is B Company's line."

"Ton me word, extraordinary place! Demned hot; walked nearly five miles. Where's the captain?"

"In his dugout, sir, near that shell-hole."

"I've got to report to him; will you tell him I'm here?"

"Hadn't you better go to him, sir?"

"Oh! Is that the thing to do?"

At that moment, unable to restrain my curiosity, I came out of my dugout, and there, sure enough, was none other than the irresistible pattern of Bond Street, Septimus D'Arcy, by all that was wonderful!

There he was, with his monocle riveted in his right eye, between the frown of his eyebrow and the chubby fatness of his cheek, with the bored expression of one who saw no reason for the necessity of the fatigue which caused the undignified beads of perspiration to assemble on an otherwise unruffled countenance. A pair of kid gloves, buttoned together, were hanging from the belt of his Sam Brown, and four inches of a blue-bordered silk handkerchief dangled from his sleeve. As he approached he half carried on his arm and half dragged along the ground, the burden that was known as his full marching order.

"Hello, Septimus!" I said, as he came along, dragging his things behind him.

"Ah! Hellow! Well, I'm demned! Never expected to find you here; awfully glad to meet you again."

"What are you doing here?"

"I'll be demned if I know! Uninteresting spot this — what?"

"Well, what have you come here for?"

"Nothing much. I saw a fellow in that big dugout in the valley, and he told me to report to you. The fact is, you know, you are attached to me, or I'm attached to you, or something of that sort."

"Well, you are not in Havre now; there are snipers about, and if you stand up there like that, you'll get hit."

"You don't mean to say so; that seems perfectly safe."

"Well, get down, and don't be a fool."

He carefully got down into the trench, leaving his equipment behind, probably hoping it would get lost, and we entered the dugout.

"I must tell you, captain, I am horribly fatigued. I came through the guns; very interesting and all that, but it's made my head ache."

"Have some water. It's rather muddy, but better than nothing these days."

"No, thanks; doctor warned me against drinking dirty water; dysentery and all that, don't you know. Any whisky and soda?"

"Look here, Septimus, now you are here, you must drop that nonsense."

"All right, old thing. I rather doubted the soda, but thank Heaven I've got a flask; a sort of emergency ration. Help yourself and lets drink it neat."

"How long have you been in the army, Septimus?"

"Three months. Why?"

"Like it?"

"Not bad. Saluting seems rather absurd; but it seems to please some. I longed to come out; thought it would be interesting and all that sort of thing. But so far I've had nothing to do but get from place to place, carrying a beastly load with me."

"Probably your own fault. I have never seen a pack or haversack crammed so full. What have you brought with you?"

"Necessaries; but not half what I shall need. Has my kit arrived?"

"My dear chap, you will never see your kit up here; and what is more, you will have to leave most of those things you have brought with you behind, before you go up the front line. Dump your things out here, and I will tell you what to take."

We emptied his pack and haversack. I have never in all my life seen such a lot of rubbish in the war kit of a soldier. There seemed to be nothing there he would really need; but a curious mixture of strange articles which would fill a fancy bazaar. There were hair-brushes with ebony backs and silver monograms, silk handkerchiefs with fancy borders, a pinky tooth-paste, oozing out of a leaden tube; and crushed between a comb and a pair of silk socks, a large bottle of reddish tooth-wash, sufficient to last him three years; and half of which had leaked through the cork to the destruction of about a dozen silk handkerchiefs, spotted and bordered in fanciful shades. There was a box of cigars, a heavy china pot of massage-cream, a pot of hair-pomade, a leather writing-case, a large ivory-backed mirror, which had lost its usefulness for ever, a bottle of fountain-pen ink, two suits of silk pajamas, one striped with pink and the other blue, a huge bath towel, a case containing seven razors, one for each day in the week, and a sponge as big as his head. Poor Septimus! in his simplicity and ignorance, for the first time in his life he had packed his own kit.

CHAPTER XI
DEATH VALLEY

MOVING OVER BATTLE-FIELDS
—— BATTALION
LONDON REGIMENT
IN POSSESSION
THE MYSTERY TRENCH
FALFEMONT FARM

THE FINAL PREPARATIONS completed, the first platoon began to move off; other platoons followed at intervals, the column slowly wending its way through the Valley of Death to its mysterious destination.

We seemed to be going into the unknown; the air was full of mystery; it was uncanny, unnatural. We were moving over battle-fields. The ground was a mass of shell-holes; progress could only be made by walking in single file along a narrow footpath, which twisted in tortuous persistency between the shell-holes, causing innumerable halts and starts, until the column tailed off into an endless line of shadowy figures.

Here and there the men became lost to view in some gun-ridden cavity; whilst there again they appeared silhouetted against the moonlit sky, as man by man they appeared and disappeared from view over a rise in the ground.

Those who had fallen in the desperate struggle of the previous week lay yet unburied. Friend and foe alike shared the shelter of the heavens, clutching at the soil of France in the agonies of death. There are times when the sight of death excuses the quivering step and the irrepressible sob from the hearts of those who pass onward to brave a similar fate.

The Valley of Death was a silent tomb of the wrath of nations, that long, winding Valley of Death, where the bodies of friend and foe lay side by side, or clutched in a desperate embrace, marked the line where the fury of nations found its expression, like the scar of a devil's vengeance.

As I looked on the bodies of the dead, twisted and mutilated, limbless and torn, some half buried in debris — here and there lying doubled in unnatural positions, while others yet, seemed to be clutching at some mortal wound — I felt like one who fearfully treads into the vortex of Dante's inferno. Yes, this was the devil's own hell, but a hell far more dreadful than I had ever imagined it to be.

After a tiring, disheartening trudge, we found the spot we were to occupy, and, to our intense relief, the — Battalion, London Regiment, were in possession. After the usual formalities of the relieving and taking over of the line of shell-holes which marked the position, I stopped for a final word with one of the — officers:

"How many casualties?" I asked.

"About fifty in two days — bit tough, eh?"

"Been attacked, then?"

"No; shelled like billyho. They've got the range nicely."

"Where's the Boche?"

"Don't quite know; somewhere in front. About eight hundred yards away there's a trench which forms three sides of a square, each side about three hundred yards, with the open side resting on Leuze Wood, and the lower end extending into the wood."

"Fritz there?"

"In the upper part, yes; but the lower part is a bit of a mystery. The part that extends into the wood the — Regiment are holding; but the rest of it the Boche seems to have. At least, that's what I think. Awkward position! Well, cheer oh!"

After a sleepless night I anxiously waited the rising mist to take a view of my surroundings. There, on the right, was a high table-land, with a frowning bluff overlooking the town of Combos, which slowly emerged, house by house, from the rising mist.

In the trench the right man of my company was vigorously shaking the hand of a French soldier, who marked the left of the French army.

There, straight in front, could be faintly seen the trench formed in

51

the shape of a square, and left of it Leuze Wood. But what were those peculiar stumps to the left of our trenches? They looked like the remains of a copse which had been shelled until only the stumps of a few trees remained. And where was Falfemont Farm? There was no sign of it anywhere. I was not sure of my position on the map; it was puzzling.

I went over to consult the French officer on my right:

"Morning, monsieur," I said, approaching a smart young officer.

"Ah! Good morning; you relieve the — Battalion, London Regiment, already — yes?"

"Yes; last night. I came to ask you what those stumps are over there; they are not marked on the map. Do you happen to know?"

"Ah! Oui; zat is Falfemont Farm. Nothing left now; very bad place that farm. Zay say one whole brigade of infantry was lost in storming that farm. Yes, nasty place, that farm, M. le Capitaine."

I went back to my trench. I didn't like the look of things. If Falfemont Farm got blown to smithereens like that, what chance did I stand? Whew! I was getting the wind up.

CHAPTER XII
OUT IN NO MAN'S LAND

SUDDEN ORDERS
THE BEGINNING OF A GREAT ADVENTURE
DIGGING IN

AFTER A STRENUOUS day's work, during which I had only time to take a mouthful of bread and cheese, which I carried in my pocket, I espied an orderly making his way towards me.

"The C.O. sent me, sir; you're wanted at once."

"Oh! any news?"

"I think we are in for a binge, sir."

"Which is the way to headquarters?"

"About two hundred yards back. Follow that narrow little track which winds around the shell holes, and you can't miss it. Don't leave the track, or you will lose your way."

On arriving at H.Q. I found a small group of officers bending anxiously over a map. The C.O. turned to me as I approached: "Ah! There you are. Get your books out, and take down your orders — ready! You are to take command of B Company. Well, now, here's our position; there's Combles and there's Leuze Wood. Take your company out into 'No Man's Land,' and extend along a line facing half right to our present position, with your left resting on the wood. C Company will be in the wood on your left; and A Company will be on your right — understand?"

"Yes, sir."

"You'll dig in to-night, and to-morrow we are going to take that trench that's formed like a square, to prepare the way for a frontal attack on Combles by the French. You'll take the upper portion of that perpendicular trench, passing the wood on your left."

"Then, I shall have to cross over the lower trench; isn't that occupied, sir?"

"The battalion bombers will clear that out for you during the night."

"When is zero hour, sir?"

"Don't know; I've told you all I know at present. Take ten flares, and send up two when you arrive at your objective, and send up another two at 6 o'clock the following morning."

"What about ammunition and water, sir?"

"The water you've already got is supposed to last forty-eight hours. I don't know about ammunition; I think there's an ammunition dump in the wood, but I will find that out and let you know. All right; it's dark enough now."

Sch! — Crash! — Zug! A 5.9 burst on the parapet a few yards away. The thud of an awky bit was felt in our midst, and the sergeant major jumped up, holding his foot. The C.O. looked up without turning a hair:

"Any one hurt?" he asked.

"Only my boots, sir," replied the sergeant major, suspiciously feeling his heel.

I took my departure and began to grope around in the dark in search of the narrow track which would guide me back to my company. I searched for about ten minutes, but in vain, and I became for a while hopelessly lost in a mass of shell-holes. I knew the direction roughly, but direction was of little use in that wild confusion of broken ground and debris.

What if I should be lost all night? What would they think? It would be put down to funk. A cold perspiration came over me. I felt an overwhelming sense of loneliness amidst that gruesome scene of destruction; and to crown it all, a feeling of responsibility and anxiety which made the craters seem deeper as I frantically scrambled out of one and into another. At last, to my intense relief, I found the little footpath and reached my trench safely.

Time was getting on. I gave orders for the men to dress and lie flat on the parados, ready for the word to move. When all preparations were completed, and bombs, picks, and shovels issued to each man, I signalled the advance, and with a few scouts in front and on the flanks, we slowly moved in single file into the unknown.

It was a pitch-black night, intensified by a slight fog, and I took my direction by compass bearing, wondering all the while if it would lead me right.

The men marched in silence. Nothing could be heard but the muffled footsteps over the soft ground, and occasional jingling of a spade or pick against the butt of a rifle.

Distance became exaggerated, and fifty paces seemed like five hundred, until I began to get a horrible fear that my compass had misled me, and that countless German eyes were watching me leading my men into the midst of their guns. Where were we going? When would we get back, and how many of us? Call it funk or what you like, but whatever it is, it's a devilishly creepy feeling; and when at last I found myself close to the edge of the wood, I felt as if I were arriving home.

But the real job had not yet begun. I signalled the halt to the leading file, and passed the word to turn to the right and extend two paces to the right and lie down. I next ordered a sentry group, consisting of one section to be sent out by each platoon to occupy shell-holes fifty yards in front as a protection against surprise.

The platoon on the left was to bend its flank to face the edge of the wood, and get in touch with C Company in the wood; while the platoon on the right secured connection with A Company. One Lewis-gun section took up position on the left flank at the corner of the wood, whilst the other Lewis gun protected my right.

These precautions against surprise being completed, I ordered the men to dig for all they were worth; rifles with bayonets fixed, and magazines charged to be placed within arm's reach at the back of the trench, the earth to be thrown in front until the parapet became bullet-proof.

I spotted one man leaning on his shovel, and looking vacantly into the darkness.

"Dig, man! Don't stand looking about you," I whispered hoarsely.

"The ground's hard, sir; it's all chalk here."

"Don't be a fool! Dig! I tell you we may be discovered any minute. If we get shelled you'll be glad enough of a hole to lie in."

Passing along the line, I overheard two men talking in an undertone:

"How do you like it, Timmy?"

"Fed to the teeth. It's all very well for the skipper to say: 'Dig like hell!' — Seems quiet enough here."

"Heard about Bill? Went balmy just after we started. He began by laughing and crying; he was as mad as a hatter. He nearly put the wind up us in the rear. The skipper sent him back with a couple of stretcher-bearers."

"Poor old Bill, hard luck. Thought he couldn't stand much. Got any water?"

"Not a drop; I'm as dry as a brick."

"Shut up; there's the skipper standing there."

The conversation stopped; but the latter part worried me not a little. Water-bottle empty, good Lord! and no more water for forty-eight hours.

All of a sudden the sky was illuminated. Half a dozen Very lights went up in rapid succession: we were discovered!

A moment or two later from two different points, three reds and a green light went up, falling in our direction. Every man stopped work and looked up in amazement. We were in for it; we wanted no telling.

"Dig like hell!" I whispered hoarsely, hurrying along the line of wondering men.

But they wanted no urging this time, and every man set to work with feverish energy.

Then the bombardment commenced, and in a few minutes the air was filled with whistling shells, screeching through the night and making the darkness hideous.

We were only a foot below the surface of the ground. Once again I hastened along the line:

"Dig like hell!"

Lights were going up in rapid succession, and the German line whence they came appeared only a couple of hundred yards in front, and seemed to form a semicircle around my left flank.

Clack! Clack! Clack! What was that? — Rifles! My sentry groups were firing. Again the rattle of rifles, this time all along the line of sentry groups.

"Stand to!"

Every man seized his rifle and crouched in the pit he had dug and faced his front. We waited: the bombardment had stopped, and the crack of the rifles alone disturbed the night.

I drew my revolver and waited in breathless suspense for the sudden rush which seemed imminent.

Were our preparations to be nipped in the bud, after all? Would it be a sudden rush; a desperate hand-to-hand fight? — and then, what then?

The minutes passed like hours in an agony of suspense, and then, unable to bear the strain any longer, I crept cautiously forward into the inky darkness towards one of the sentry groups to find out what was amiss.

"Halt! Who is there?"

"O. C. B Company."

"Advance!"

"What's up?" I asked, sliding into the shell hole beside the corporal.

"There seemed to be a patrol moving about in front; it's all quiet now, sir."

"All right; double the sentries for the next hour."

I returned to the line and ordered the men to continue digging.

The bombardment continued, but by and by we began to grow accustomed to the din. Several casualties occurred; but still the work of digging in continued.

Time was getting on, and I must make my plans for to-morrow's attack.

A few minutes later I chanced to notice a figure sitting leisurely in a shell-hole.

"Why, Septimus, is that you?"

"I think so; I say, I think so. Unearthly row; devilishly dangerous place, this — what?"

"But what are you doing in there?"

"I was just coming to talk to you about ammunition. A shell burst, and my face is simply covered with dust. Has the ammunition arrived yet?"

"No; there's an ammunition dump in the wood somewhere."

"Like me to go and find it?"

I looked at him in amazement. It wasn't funk then, that made him seek safety in that shell-hole. Was it possible that dear old Septimus, this bland, indifferent tubby, blasé old thing of Bond Street, was anxious to go into that creepy, mysterious wood to look for ammunition?

"All right; take a corporal and 12 men, and bring back six boxes. Don't take unnecessary risks; we shall need every man tomorrow."

Septimus sprang out of the shell-hole, saluted in the most correct manner — something quite new for him — and disappeared in the darkness.

This was a new side of Septimus's character which had not shown itself before. Only the stoutest heart would have chosen to wander about in that wood at midnight, with enemy patrols lurking about. Septimus was a man, after all.

Five minutes later he passed me, leading his men. He gripped my hand as he passed, with the remark: "Well! Ta-ta, old thing."

"Cheer oh!"

And Septimus was gone. We may call men fops, simple vacant fools, or what we like; but the war has proved over and over again that the man within the man is merely disguised by his outer covering. Many a Bond Street Algy, or ballroom idol has proved amidst the terrors of war that the artificial covering of a peace-time habit is but skin-deep; and the real man is underneath.

CHAPTER XIII

A NIGHT OF ALARM

SEPTIMUS IN A NEW ROLE
SAVING THE AMMUNITION
THE LAST CARTRIDGE

JUST THEN A movement in the rear of my position attracted my attention. A number of men were approaching; then halting, they sat on the ground, while two figures continued on towards me.

They were Second Lieutenant Wade, the intrepid scout officer, and Second Lieutenant Brady, in command of the battalion bombers.It was Brady who spoke first: "Hullo! Getting peppered pretty hot, aren't you?"

"Rather lively! Where are you off to?"

"I've got orders to bomb out that mysterious trench you've heard so much about, in order to clear the way for your attack to-morrow. I'm going in front of your line and along the edge of the wood."

I despatched a runner to warn the sentry groups, and presently the little group of bombers disappeared round the edge of the wood into the darkness on their adventurous errand, the success of which would mean so much to me on the morrow.

All this time the work of digging is continued with unabated anxiety, shells dropping around unceasingly.

All of a sudden I was startled by a rattle of musketry in the direction of the wood. There was silence; then several more shots followed by a rushing, tearing noise, and yells.

Almost at the same moment the ammunition party emerged breathlessly from the wood.

I ran forward to where the men were dropping the ammunition boxes on the ground, and falling exhausted. For a moment or two they were too breathless to speak. I counted the men: there were 12 of them, and the six boxes of ammunition had safely arrived.

But where were Septimus and the corporal? All was silent in the wood. I turned to the nearest man who was by this time sitting up, holding his head in his hands.

"Where is Mr. D'Arcy and Corporal Brown?" I asked.

"God knows, sir! They stayed to cover our retirement."

"What happened?"

"We found the ammunition dump, sir, and were just beginning to move the boxes when we heard some one moving. We grabbed our rifles and waited. There seemed to be quite a number crawling around us. Mr. D'Arcy ordered us to retire at once, and get the ammunition away at any cost; he said he would stay behind and cover our retreat, and Corporal Brown offered to stay with him. We hadn't got far, sir, when they opened fire; bullets hit the trees and whizzed over our heads. Then we heard a rush and some yells. I distinctly heard something in German, and Mr. D'Arcy's voice shout back: 'Kamarade be damned!' Then there was a scuffle; that's all I know."

My heart beat wildly as I listened to this story. Good God! what did that silence mean? There was no further time to be lost.

I ordered a relief party and led the way into the wood. There was not a sound to be heard as we crept forward on our hands and knees towards the spot where the ammunition had been found.

What was that? We listened breathlessly, and again we heard a low groan almost in our midst. There was a shell-hole just in front, and crawling along on all fours, I found Septimus D'Arcy, wounded and helpless, with his left leg almost blown away, and bleeding from the head.

"What's up, D'Arcy? What has happened?" I whispered hoarsely.

A faint smile of recognition came over his pale face as I supported him in my arms. His words came painfully:

"The ammunition — is it — safe?" "Yes, quite safe."

"But what happened after they left?" "I stayed behind — with the corporal — to protect their retirement. We opened rapid fire — to draw German fire on to us. I saw six creeping forward. They called to us — to surrender. I refused — demn them! They threw bombs — killed the

60

corporal — dirty dogs! smashed my leg — nothing much. I picked off three — with my revolver — never used beastly thing before; two bolted — last one jumped at me — with bayonet. That's him there — just got him — last cartridge."

Septimus was lying heavily on my arms. Nothing could be done for him; I saw the end was at hand.

"Good-bye, captain! Knew you'd come. Don't know much about soldiering — good sport; shan't have to carry that — demned pack again."

A placid smile came over his chubby face as he gasped out the last words. His monocle was still firmly fixed between his fat cheek and his eyebrow. Once more he seemed indifferent to his surroundings.

In front of him, the silent evidence of his plucky stand, were the dead bodies of four Germans. By his side lay a revolver. I picked up and examined the chamber; the last cartridge had been fired!

The men had gathered around; their caps were off. Septimus seemed to be looking up smilingly into their faces.

Septimus was dead! But Septimus was still in Bond Street!

CHAPTER XIV
NEXT MORNING

A COUNCIL OF WAR
OPERATION ORDERS
A BITTER DISAPPOINTMENT

THREE A.M. HEAVY shell-fire still continues. I have just ordered the men to cease work and take rest. Trench is about two feet deep; men are dead beat.

4 A.M. Have just received three pages of operation orders. We are to attack at 4.45 P.M. in four ways, starting from the trenches we have been digging, and advancing diagonally from the corner of the wood across the open; passing over the mystery trench and taking the central trench.

I have only a vague idea at present where that is. Am fervently hoping that the battalion bombers have solved the mystery trench and cleared it. No news from them yet. God knows what has been happening there during the night.

5 A.M. Have just held a council of war with my officers and N. C. O.'s, and explained in detail my plans for the attack. Very impressive sight, seeing them all crouching around me in a shell hole, with shells bursting around us, while they listened intently to my orders.

"Each officer is to carry his papers in lower right-hand hip pocket; and if he fails, the nearest man is to search the pocket and hand the contents on to the next senior. I intend to attack in the following order:

First wave	No. 5 Platoon
Second	No. 6 Platoon
Third	No. 7 Platoon and
Fourth wave	No. 8 Platoon

Eighty yards interval between each wave. Bombing sections of Nos. 5 and 7 to be on the right, and Nos. 6 and 8 on the left of their respective platoons.

"No. 1 Lewis Gun to be on the right of the second wave; No. 2 Lewis Gun to be on the left of the fourth wave.

"Two runners from each platoon to report to me five minutes before zero hour. My position, accompanied by the runners, will be between the third and fourth wave.

"On arrival at objective Lewis Gunners to establish strong points, assisted by bombers at each end of objective. Each man to carry two hundreds rounds of ammunition and three bombs; also three sand-bags in his belt, and a pick or shovel tucked through his belt behind. Bombers to carry each a sack, containing twelve bombs, but no tools."

Strange warfare this, going into a fight like a navvy.

5.30 A.M. Plans have been explained in detail to every man, and orders given that if all officers and N. C. O.'s are knocked out, the men are to carry on and finish the job themselves.

Very foggy morning; we are able to finish digging trench.

6 A.M. Astounding news. The battalion bombers have failed. A few survivors, after fighting all night, have been driven into the wood. The mystery trench over which I must cross is in the hands of the Boches. Could we hope to accomplish the double task?

The men heard the news in silence.

7 A.M. Breakfast consists of some dirty bread and cheese, and a little water.

8. A.M. Fog lifted. Our position is correct. Can see objective plainly about four hundred yards off. We can also be seen plainly, and snipers are busy trying to pick us off.

Have made a reconnaissance, and find intervening ground a mass of shell-holes. Looks like a rough sea. The advance will be difficult; the ground is so churned up. Not a square yard of unbroken ground.

2. P.M. Everything is now in readiness, with nearly three hours to spare.

Have ordered men to eat their dinners, which consists of bread and cheese at 3 P.M., so that they will go into the fight on full stomachs.

I have had no sleep or proper food for nearly two days. Will lie down and get an hour's rest before the attack.

CHAPTER XV

THE ADVANCE THROUGH LEUZE WOOD

NEW OPERATION ORDERS
"AT ANY COST"
LIKE RATS IN A TRAP

I HAD HARDLY closed my eyes when a runner from headquarters came hurrying along the line, and was directed to where I was dozing at the bottom of a trench.

"Message from the C. O., sir, very urgent."

I signed the receipt and tore the envelope open. Good heavens! new operation orders! I was astounded. I looked again, hardly daring to believe my eyes. Sure enough, there was no mistake about it, three pages of closely written operation orders. The head-line seemed to be mocking me:

"Fresh operation orders, cancelling those issued this morning."

I read on: "You are to advance on through Leuze Wood, and attack from that part of the wood which forms the fourth side of the square shaped trench, thus attacking the inside of the square; B Company taking the lower half, and C Company the upper half; A Company to be in support."

A cold shiver ran down my back. What a calamity! and after all the pains I had taken to work out the details of the attack, and that dreadful night spent in digging these trenches to jump off from. Every man knew what to do, and now at the eleventh hour the whole plan was altered.

I glanced again at the new orders:

"You are to be at the new place of assembly by 3.30 P.M.; zero hour is 4.45."

I looked at my watch — Great Scott! it was already 2.15; at 3 P.M. I must commence the advance through the wood.

The men had not yet commenced their dinners. What time was there? and how was it possible to sit down quietly and digest those three pages of new orders and understand their meaning? What time had I to make new plans and explain to each man his new task?

There was not a moment to be lost; I turned to my two runners:

"Dinners to be eaten at once. Platoon commanders wanted at the double."

I waited, and by and by the platoon commanders, Second Lieutenant Farman and Chislehirst, and Sergeants Blackwell and Barnes, came running along the top, snipers shooting at them as they ran along. They halted on the parados, saluting as they came up, and, still standing up, awaited orders, seemingly indifferent to the excellent target which they presented.

"Lie down flat," I ordered.

They did as I directed, their faces turned anxiously toward me, wondering what was up.

"New operation orders just arrived from headquarters; previous orders cancelled. We are to advance through the wood and attack from the inside of the square."

I hurriedly read the whole of the orders over to them, and they listened silently.

"Go back to your platoons. The men are to be dressed in battle order by 2.50 — it's now 2.30 — by 3 p.m the platoons are to be closed up along the trench, and the leading platoon will enter the wood in single file, other platoons following."

As I glanced up I noticed their faces were pale; they were listening intently, but uttering no sound. They were receiving orders; they realised their responsibility, and they knew their duty.

The last paragraph was underlined. I hurriedly read it and looked up at them again:

"Just one more thing," I said. "These are my orders underlined: YOU MUST REACH YOUR OBJECTIVE AT ANY COST. IF DRIVEN BACK, YOU ARE TO MAKE A STAND AT THE EDGE OF THE WOOD, AND HOLD OUT TILL THE LAST MAN FALLS."

It sounded like a death sentence, a forecast of the hour of trial which we were to face. Only those who have received such orders on the field of battle can realise what it feels like.

In those few dramatic moments we counted our lives as lost. We recognised how desperate was our task. Success we might hope for; but failure we must pay the price of. We must fight till the last man falls — and yet we were merely civilian soldiers.

I looked into their faces; our eyes met. I understood; I could trust them; they could trust me.

"That's all; return to your platoons and prepare to move."

They had not uttered a word through all this; no words were necessary. They jumped to their feet; saluted as though we were back on Salisbury Plain, and the next moment ran along the parados to their platoons.

I watched them, and saw them kneel down on the top of their trench, indifferent to the snipers' bullets whistling about their heads, hurriedly explaining the situation to their men.

By 3 P.M. the men were ready and had closed along the trench to the wood.

The movement had been seen by the enemy, and a terrific burst of firing commenced; although, at the time I could not see what effect it was having.

I waited several minutes, but there was no further movement along the trench to indicate that the first platoon had entered the wood. I sent forward the message, "Carry on," but still no movement resulted.

At last, feeling something was wrong and unable to restrain my impatience any longer, I jumped out of the trench and ran along the parados.

What I saw there appalled me for the moment; the wood in front of me was filled with bursting shells; a continuous pr-r-r-r seemed to be moving backward and forward, and bullets were whistling in all directions.

Good God! what a hell! No wonder the men hesitated! What was to be done? My orders left me no alternative. I must advance through the wood. My brain kept repeating the words, "At any cost!" What a cost it would be to enter that hell! It was now, or never!

We were hesitating; something must be done, and done quickly. I looked at Farman, and I knew I could count on him.

The next moment I leaped into a newly made shell-hole, about five yards in the wood; called upon Farman to follow, and a moment later he came jumping after.

The noise was terrific. We yelled at the top of our voices for the next man to follow.

The next man to take the leap was the company sergeant-major. A piece of shell struck him in the side, and he rolled over on the ground, clutching at his tunic.

Again we yelled for the men to come along; and one by one they took the leap.

When six of us were in the shell-hole it was time for us to empty it to make room for others. Farman and I took it in turns to lead the way, and this process went on through the wood, leaping from hole to hole, and yelling at the top of our lungs for the others to follow us.

By this time the scene inside the wood was indescribable. Machine-gun bullets were spraying backward and forward; 6 -inch shells were exploding in all directions; and the din was intensified by the crashing of trees uprooted by the explosions, and the dull thud of the missiles striking the ground.

Through the dull light of that filthy wood we frequently cast an anxious glance towards the red rockets being sent up from the German lines, directing the fire of their artillery towards us.

Sometimes, in leaping forward, we would land beside the dead and mutilated carcass of a German soldier who had fallen a week before. It was ghastly, terrible; and the millions of flies sucking at his open wounds would swarm about us, seemingly in a buzz of anger at our disturbance. But sickly and ghastly as the scene was, farther and farther into this exaggerated hell we must go.

By this time the cries of the wounded added to the terrors of the scene. Each time we jumped into a shell-hole, we turned to watch the men leap in. Each time it seemed that a new face appeared, and the absence of those who had jumped into the last shell-hole was only too significant.

But, undaunted by their falling comrades, each man, in his turn, leaped forward and would lie gasping for breath until his turn came for another effort.

Farman was the first to speak. It was his turn to take the next leap:

"I don't think it really matters. There's a hole about thirty yards away; I think I'll go straight for that."

He got up and walked leisurely across, as though inviting the death which seemed inevitable. He stopped at the shell-hole, and for a moment seemed to be looking down undecided whether to jump in or not.

I shouted at him:

"Don't be a damned fool; jump!"

The next moment a shell burst between us, and I fell back into the shell-hole. When I again looked out and my eyes could penetrate the smoke, I saw no sign of Farman. I yelled, and to my intense relief I saw his head appear. He was safe!

Again and again the last paragraph of my orders seemed to be blazing in front of me, and like a hidden hand from that dark inferno of horrors, kept beckoning me forward, "At any cost! At any cost!"

Yes; this must be the end; but it's hell to die in a wood.

The men used to call it Lousy Wood. What do they call it now? They were brave fellows; and they were only civilian soldiers, too! They used to be volunteers once. People would laugh, and call them Saturday afternoon soldiers.

Reviews in Hyde Park used to be a joke, and the comic papers caricatured these men, and used them as material for their jests.

They were only Territorials! That man, panting hard at the bottom of the shell-hole, and still clutching at his rifle, is a bank clerk; that man who fell at the last jump, with his stomach ripped up, was a solicitor's clerk.

Look at the others. Their faces are pale; their eyes are bulging. But they are the same faces one used to see in Cornhill and Threadneedle Street.

Yes, they are only Territorials! But here in this filthy wood they are damned proud of it.

And what is taking place in England to-day?

Is it really true that while all this is going on in Leuze Wood, orchestras are playing sweet music in brilliantly lighted restaurants in London — while a gluttonous crowd eat of the fat of the land? Is it really true that women in England are dressing more extravagantly than ever? Is it really true that some men in England are unable or unwilling to share the nation's peril — are even threatening to strike?

No! No! Do not let us think that this is the true picture of England. If it is, then, Territorials, let us die in Leuze Wood!

CHAPTER XVI
THE ATTACK

A DESPERATE SITUATION
BATTLE FORMATION
"FOR ENGLAND"

JOY! THE LAST leap I took landed me in a trench, and I found to my great relief that it was the lower part of the square which ran through the wood. A few yards along this trench it emerged into the open, where it was in possession of the Germans.

Farman and I sat down, side by side, breathing heavily from our exertions.

"That was hell, Farman," I said, hardly daring to trust my voice.

"Awful!"

"I hope the men are still following."

"Those that are left."

"Have a cigarette; it will buck the men up to see us smoking."

"Thanks, I will, though I'm as dry as a bone."

"Save your water; we've still got the attack to do. We've got an hour yet; that will give the men time to recover."

By this time, one by one, the men began to jump into the trench. As the men arrived, their faces pale and eyes started, we called them by name. They looked up and smiled with relief at seeing us sitting there, side by side. They recognised that the last jump had been made, and for the time being, at any rate, they were safe.

We had started through the wood, about one hundred and thirty strong, and barely eighty mustered for the final attack.

Some men of C Company appeared, threading their way along the trench. Farther in the wood, the commander, Lieutenant Barton, came up to arrange details for the attack.

"You got your new orders in time, then," I remarked.

"Just in time. It's hell, isn't it? I've lost heavily already, and we've still got to go over the top."

"I've got orders to take half the battalion bombers from you; where are they?"

"I would like to keep them; there are not many left, and they are badly broken up — been fighting all night."

"All right, you keep them. I'm going to form up between here and that broken tree. Will you form up farther to the left?"

"All right. Well, I'll be off; cheer oh! old chap."

"Good-bye, Barton. Good luck!"

I never saw Barton again! I heard some months afterwards that he fell, riddled with machine-gun bullets whilst leading his men into the subsequent attack.

"Pass the word for No. 8 Platoon commander," I ordered, wishing to ascertain if the last platoon had arrived.

A young sergeant came up at the double, and saluted.

"I am in command, sir."

His tone and manner inspired me immensely. Notwithstanding all the danger we had passed through, he seemed to be full of ginger and pride at finding himself in command of the platoon.

"Where is Mr. Chislehirst, then?" I asked.

"Wounded, sir, in the wood; shot through the chest. The last I saw of him he was giving another wounded man a drink from his water bottle."

"All right; do you understand your orders?"

"Yes, sir, quite."

"Return to your platoon, and await orders to form up."

He saluted and doubled back to his men. I forget his name, but he was a fine fellow, that sergeant; quite cool, and evidently pleased at his new responsibility.

So poor old Chislehirst was hit; fine fellow; very young, only about twenty; good company in the mess; reliable in the field. Just like him to give his water-bottle to some one else when he could go no farther.

Farman was my only subaltern left. Suddenly he gripped my arm and pointed into the wood:

"Look over there. Who are those fellows creeping along that trench?"

I looked in the direction he was pointing, and there, to my astonishment, on the very ground just vacated by C Company, about a dozen figures in bluish grey were creeping along a shallow trench. I thought at first they were coming in to surrender; but they made no signs, but were evidently making the best of cover.

What were they up to? There were only about 12 of them, and I had between 70 and 80 men. For such a small number to come out alone and attack us seemed absurd, and I waited, expecting them to throw up their hands and come in. Perhaps they thought they had not been seen. I picked up a rifle, and taking aim, fired at the last man but one; I missed.

Still they kept creeping on. I fired a second time at the same man, and he dropped. The thing didn't seem real, seeing those heads bobbing along a trench; I felt for a moment as though I were shooting rabbits.

The next moment I realised their object. By this time they had worked well round my flanks. They were evidently a few daring men, who were trying to creep up unnoticed, with the intention of throwing bombs while we were in a congested area, occupied in forming up for the attack. A daring ruse, but a clever one; for a dozen men throwing bombs at close quarters could wipe us off the map, or, at any rate, could do enough damage by shock action of this kind to prevent our attack starting.

I dared not give any order to fire for fear of hitting the men of C Company. The situation was desperate. I had no time to spare, for zero hour was close at hand. The same thoughts were running through Farman's mind.

"Shall I have a go at them?" he said.

"Yes; form up your platoon, and stick them with the bayonet; then join the attack as a fourth wave."

I watched Farman and his platoon with bayonets fixed, creeping on all fours towards the German bombers. That was the last I saw of them, as it was within 10 minutes of zero hour, and we were not yet in battle formation.

I heard afterwards that they did the job well. But to part with the platoon and my only remaining officer at this critical moment was a great loss to me; for I could not count upon them in the attack for which I had now only three platoons left — about sixty men.

Half my strength had gone, and the real attack had not yet begun. I sent for the remaining platoon commanders and explained the situation:

"No. 6 Platoon will now become the first wave. Form up and extend along the edge of the wood and await my signal to advance into the open. No. 7 Platoon, form up immediately in rear; and No. 8 Platoon, assemble in the trench close up. Bombing section of No. 6 will proceed along the trench parallel with the advance, bombing it out as they go along."

The men formed up. The minutes seemed to be like hours. We were facing the inside of the square trench, which was a mass of shell-holes, and as though anticipating our intention, shells were bursting and bullets whistling on all sides.

How peaceful England must be at this moment; how pretty the villages! And how wicked this hell seemed in front of us! And these were the men of England — nice chaps, only Territorials.

One used to meet them in the city every day. Some were awful nuts. See them at lunch; watch them pouring out of Liverpool Street Station between 9 and 10 o'clock in the morning, with newspaper and walking-stick; see them in the banks, bending over ledgers. You could hardly believe it; but these were the same men.

They were not very trim just now; their hands are grimy as they clutch at their rifles, undaunted by the terrors they have already passed through and the sight of their fallen comrades left groaning in the wood.

There they are, extended and lying flat on the ground, waiting further orders. They have come through one hell by the skin of their teeth, and are patiently looking into another hell; their lives were counted by minutes, these office men. But their eyes were fixed on the far side of the square trench which was to be their objective; unless by God's will, and for the sake of England, they found an earlier one.

London men! Some may call you "only Territorials." Training has been your hobby; but fighting was never your profession.

What will England think of this? England may never know.

Who ever heard of Leuze Wood before? If a man is killed in England there is an inquest. People read about it in the papers.

Are the people left behind in England suffering hardships uncomplainingly, and gritting their teeth like you are? You are only getting a bob a day. England needs you; you are masters. Why don't you strike at this critical moment?

No, my lads; you are made of different stuff. You are men! There are those in England this day who work for England's cause; there are others who are enriching themselves by your absence; there are homes which will feel your sacrifice.

You have seen the wasted homes and the ghastly outrages in France; and between that picture and the green fields of England you must make your stand; those in England will depend upon you this day.

Zero hour is at hand. Agonies, mutilation, and death are within a few yards of you. There will be no pictures of your deeds; there are no flags or trumpets to inspire you; you are lying on the dirty ground on the edge of Leuze Wood, with hell in front of you, and hell behind you — hell in those trenches on the left, hell in those trenches on the right.

One more minute and you will stand up and walk into it. My lads! It's for England!

CHAPTER XVII
AT ANY COST

OVER THE TOP
MAD, FIGHTING MAD
THE FINAL ASSAULT

A T LAST THE thunder of our guns towards the German lines confirmed the hour. Zero hour had arrived; the barrage had begun.

"No. 6 Platoon will advance."

The front line jumped up and walked into the open. Wonderful! Steady as a rock! The line was perfect.

On the left the front line of C Company has also emerged from the wood; the bombers of No. 6 Platoon disappeared along the mystery trench.

The tut-ut-ut-ut of machine-guns developed from several parts of the square, while the crack of rifles increased in intensity.

No. 7 Platoon jumped up and advanced into the open, followed by the third wave.

I extended my runners and followed.

What followed next beggars description. As I write these lines my hand hesitates to describe the hell that was let loose upon those men. No eye but mine could take in the picture so completely.

Will the world ever know what these men faced and fought against — these men of the City of London? Not unless I tell it, for I alone saw all that happened that day; and my hand alone, weak and incapable though it feels, is the only one that can do it.

Barely had I emerged from the wood with my ten runners when a perfect hurricane of shells were hurled at us, machine-guns from several points spraying their deadly fire backward and forward, dropping men like corn before the reaper. From all three sides of the square a hurricane of fire was poured into the centre of the square upon us, as we emerged from the wood.

In far less time than it takes to record it, the attacking waves became a mere sprinkling of men. They went on for a yard or two, and then all seemed to vanish; and even my runners, whom I had extended into line, were dropping fast.

The situation was critical, desperate. Fearful lest the attack should fail, I ran forward, and collecting men here and there from shell-holes where some had taken refuge, I formed them into a fresh firing-line, and once more we pressed forward.

Again and again the line was thinned; and again the survivors, undaunted and unbeaten, reformed and pressed forward.

Men laughed, men cried in the desperation of the moment. We were grappling with death; we were dodging it, cheating it; we were mad, blindly hysterical. What did anything matter? Farther and farther into the inferno we must press, at any cost, at any cost; leaping, jumping, rushing, we went from shell-hole to shell-hole; and still the fire continued with unrelenting fury.

I jumped into a shell-hole, and found myself within ten yards of my objective. My three remaining runners jumped in alongside of me. They were Arnold, Dobson, and Wilkinson.

Arnold was done for! He looked up at me with eyes staring and face blanched, and panted out that he could go no farther, and I realised that I could count on him no more.

I glanced to the left, just in time to see three Germans not five yards away, and one after the other jump from a shell-hole which formed a sort of bay to their trench, and run away.

Wishing to save the ammunition in my revolver for the hand-to-hand scuffle which seemed imminent, I seized the rifle of Arnold and fired. I missed all three; my hand was shaky.

What was I to do next? The company on my left had disappeared; the trench just in front of me was occupied by the Boches. I had with me three runners, one of whom was helpless, and in the next shell-hole about six men, the sole survivors of my company.

Where were the supports? Anxiously I glanced back toward the wood; why did they not come?

Poor fellows, I did not know it at the time, but the hand of death had dealt with them even more heavily in the wood than it had with us.

My position was desperate. I could not retire. My orders were imperative: "You must reach your objective at any cost." I must get there somehow. But even if we got there, how long could I hope to hold out with such a handful of men?

Immediate support I must have; I must take risks. I turned to brave Dobson and Wilkinson:

"Message to the supports: 'Send me two platoons quickly; position critical.'"

Without a moment's hesitation they jumped up and darted off with the message which might save the day.

Dobson fell before he had gone two yards; three paces farther on I saw Wilkinson, the pet of the company, turn suddenly round and fall on the ground, clutching at his breast. All hope for the supports was gone.

At this moment the bombing section, which by this time had cleared the mystery trench, arrived on the right of the objective; and to my delirious joy, I noticed the Germans in the trench in front of me running away along the trench.

It was now, or never! We must charge over that strip of land and finish them with the bayonet. A moment's hesitation and the tables might again be turned, and all would be lost. The trench in front must be taken by assault; it must be done. There were six or seven of us left, and we must do it. I yelled to the men:

"Get ready to charge, they are running. Come on! Come on!"

I jumped out of the shell-hole, and they followed me. Once again I was mad. I saw nothing, I heard nothing; I wanted to kill! kill!

Pf— ung!

Oh! My God! I was hit in the head! I was blind!

CHAPTER XVIII
LEFT ON THE FIELD

THE MYSTERY OF DEATH
THE SECRET CODE
TWO TERRIBLE DAYS

I WAS WOUNDED! I was blind! But the moments that followed are clear in my memory. The brain shocked by a blow works quickly and actively in its excited effort to hold its own.

I was quite conscious and thinking clearly: I knew what had happened and what would happen; I remembered every detail.

My head at the moment was inclined to the right, for I was shouting to the men. Like a flash I remembered that about fifty yards to the left of me there was a "German strong point" still occupied by the Germans. A bullet had entered my left temple; it must have come from a sniper in that strong point. The bullet had passed clean through my head; I thought it had emerged through my right temple. I was mistaken on that point, for I found some days later that it had emerged through the centre of my right eye.

I remember distinctly clutching my head and sinking to the ground, and all the time I was thinking "so this is the end — the finish of it all; shot through the head, mine is a fatal wound."

Arnold jumped up, and catching me in his arms, helped me back into the shell-hole.

I hesitate to tell what followed. But as I am trying to record the sensations experienced at the time of receiving a head wound, I will describe the next experience simply, and leave the reader to form his own conclusions.

I was blind then, as I am now; but the blackness which was then before me underwent a change. A voice from somewhere behind me said: "This is death; will you come?"

Then gradually the blackness became more intense. A curtain seemed to be slowly falling; there was space; there was darkness, blacker than my blindness; everything was past. There was a peacefulness, a nothingness; but a happiness indescribable.

I seemed for a moment somewhere in the emptiness looking down at my body, lying in the shell hole, bleeding from the temple. I was dead! and that was my body; but I was happy.

But the voice I had heard seemed to be waiting for an answer. I seemed to exert myself by a frantic effort, like one in a dream who is trying to awaken.

I said: "No, not now; I won't die." Then the curtain slowly lifted; my body moved and I was moving it. I was alive!

There, my readers, I have told you, and I have hesitated to tell it before. More than that, I will tell you that I was not unconscious; neither did I lose consciousness until several minutes later, and then unconsciousness was quite different.

I have told you how clear was my brain the moment I was hit, and I tell you also that after the sensation I have just related, my brain was equally clear, as I will show you, until I became unconscious.

Call it a hallucination, a trick of the brain, or what you will. I make no attempt to influence you; I merely record the incident — but my own belief I will keep to myself.

Whatever it was, I no longer feel there is any mystery about death. Nor do I dread it.

Arnold was busy tearing open the field dressing which I carried in a pocket of my tunic.

"Use the iodine first, Arnold; it's in the pocket in a glass phial."

"The glass is broken, sir."

"In a piece of paper there are two morphia tablets — quick, better give them to me."

"They are not here, sir."

And he bound the dressing round my eyes as the blood trickled down my face.

"Quick, Arnold, my right pocket — feel in it; some papers there — a secret code — take them out — tear them up — quickly; tell me have you done it?"

"Yes, sir, I have done it."

I was sinking; I felt myself going; I felt that the end was at hand. I clutched his shoulder and pulled him towards me:

"Arnold, I'm going. If you get back — tell my — wife —" But the message that was on my lips was not finished; I could speak no more. I was dropping into space, dropping, dropping; everything disappeared, I remembered no more.

I do not know how long I remained in this condition. I remember gaining consciousness and finding Arnold by my side.

Something terrible was happening. I gradually began to realise that another attack was taking place over my head. This time the fire was coming from both sides. A stream of bullets seemed to be pouring over the shell-hole. The meaning was obvious: a machine-gun had been placed in the trench ten yards away, and its deadly fire was pouring over the shell-hole in which we lay. Loud explosions were taking place all round us, and with each explosion the earth seemed to upheave, and I felt the thug, thug of pieces of metal striking the earth close by; whilst showers of earth kept falling on my body. I couldn't last long. The guns of both sides seemed to be searching for us; we must soon be blown to pieces.

How long this lasted I cannot say. I was weak; my shattered nerves could not stand such a terrible ordeal. I lay huddled and shivering at the bottom of the shell-hole, waiting for the jagged metal to strike my body, or be hurled, mutilated, into the air.

Again I became unconscious. When I next recovered my senses Arnold was trying to lift me, to carry me away, but his strength was not equal to it. He laid me down again.

The firing had ceased. He seemed to be peering out of the shell-hole and talking to me. I think he was planning escape. It must have been dark, for he seemed uncertain about the direction.

Then I began to vomit; I seemed to be vomiting my heart out, while Arnold seemed to be trying to comfort me.

I again became unconscious. When I regained consciousness for the third time it seemed to me that I had been insensible for a great length of time. But I seemed to be much refreshed, although very weak.

Everything was silent, uncanny; I could see nothing, hear nothing. Yes, I remembered; I was shot blind, and I was still in the shell-hole. I felt my head; there was a rough bandage round it, covering my eyes. The bandage over my right eye was hardened with blood, and dried blood covered my left cheek. My hair was matted with clay and blood; and my clothes seemed to be covered with loose earth.

But what did this uncanny silence mean? —

Arnold, where was he? I called him by name, but there was no response. I remembered the firing I had heard: yes, he must be dead.

In my blindness and despair I groped on my hands and knees around the shell-hole to find his body. He was not there. *I was alone!*

CHAPTER XIX
THE JAWS OF DEATH

LONELINESS, DARKNESS, AND SILENCE
A LAST EFFORT
I PREPARE FOR DEATH

I DID NOT know at the time, of course, what had become of Arnold; but I found out later.

Fearing I was dying when I lapsed into unconsciousness again, after my fit of vomiting, he decided under cover of darkness to try and find his way back to the British lines to bring me aid.

After stumbling about in and out of shell holes, he suddenly saw the barrel of a rifle pointing at him from a trench close by, and following him as he moved; and a moment later he was a prisoner.

Understanding German, he told his captors that I was lying out in No Man's Land, and begged them to send me medical aid; and they answered that stretcher-bearers would be sent to make a search.

Whether the stretcher-bearers were sent or not I do not know; but if they were, they were not successful in finding me; for to the best of my belief it was on the Monday morning that I again regained consciousness, to find myself alone — two days after I had been shot.

It is difficult for me to describe my feelings when I found myself alone. I had no pain, I seemed to feel very small and the world very large. I sat up and felt my head; my face felt twice its usual size, and seemed sticky and clammy with earth and blood.

Everything was so silent.

There was a great lump of hardened blood where the rough field dressing covered my right eye; my left cheek, nose, and lips were swollen tremendously.

Whether it was night or day I did not know. But I knew I was blind. I tried to collect my thoughts and to reason out my position.

Where was the German line, and where was the British? I knew that I must be a considerable distance from the British line; but which direction it was in, I could not tell.

If I were to crawl, which way should I go and where should I find myself? Better to make the attempt and take my chance, than lie where I was. On my hands and knees I tried to crawl up the side of the shell-hole. But I had not reckoned on my weakness; the world was so large and I was so small.

Before I could reach the top my strength gave out, and I slid to the bottom. Again and again I tried, and with each attempt I kept slipping back, each time, bringing with me a pile of loose earth.

At last I realised how hopeless it all was, with so little strength. And unable even to reach to the top of the shell-hole, how could I hope ever to reach the British line across the sea of shell holes which intervened? I seemed so far from everything; though little did I dream at the time that German soldiers were within a few yards of me in the trench from which I had driven them by such desperate efforts two days before — two days! Surely it was two years!

Then my fate dawned upon me. Of course the end was quite logical. This was the end; it could not be otherwise. Had I not made up my mind it would come? Surely I did before I started? Was I not shot through the head and left to die? Well, this was the proper place to die. But what surprised me was that the thought of dying seemed so comforting. I was so weary, and death seemed so peaceful.

I have heard people say that when a person is drowning, after the first frantic struggles are over, a delightful sensation of peacefulness comes over him, and he ceases to desire to help himself. That was how I felt at that moment. This shell hole was my grave. Well, it seemed quite right and proper.

The idea of getting back to life after suffering so many deaths seemed very unreasonable. My sensations were those of one who had awakened to find himself buried alive. To be alive at all was cheating death, which held me firmly in its grip. Better to accept it and wait calmly for the end.

The life of the world seemed so far away from me. My family, my home, my friends and scenes that I used to know so well seemed in a misty past, a long, long way away — a different age.

After all, it did not matter very much. It was all so very long ago. It had all happened long ago. My absence was an accepted fact; I was now a memory.

Now, I have already said that I awoke refreshed. I will say, further, that I was never so clearheaded in my life. I had little power in my limbs. My brain was never more calm and calculating and indifferent to the death which I knew was at hand.

It was not nerve, because I had none. It had nothing to do with the question of pluck or cowardice. It was simply the state of the brain before its last kick. I had ceased to resist my fate; I accepted it. I was not dead yet — but I was to die there, and that was to be my grave.

I began to think out calmly in what way my life would nicker out, and I concluded that it would come as a result of my wound during a period of unconsciousness, or by the slower process of thirst, starvation, and exposure. In the latter case I should probably have violent spasms or struggles. I had better prepare myself.

I was lying in a very uncomfortable position. There was a pile of loose earth, which stuck against my body awkwardly. With my hands and feet I scooped it out until my body lay comfortably in a hollow, with the loose earth forming a sort of bed. In doing this I found a water bottle. Arnold must have left it behind for me. There was only a drain in it, which I drank, and threw the bottle away.

I next searched my pockets for food and found a small crust, the remains of what had been my food the day before the attack. I placed this carefully in my pocket for use at the time when I should experience the final pangs of starvation. My own water-bottle still contained about half a pint of water. I placed this on the ground, close to where my face would be, so that I could clutch it readily.

These preparations over, my brain began to get tired. There was nothing else to be done; everything was ready. I would lie down now and wait for the end. I laid my head on the ground, using the side of the shell-hole as a pillow.

I was very comfortable, the soft earth seemed almost like a bed. After all, I was a lucky fellow to be able to die in a comfortable way like this. I wondered how long it would really be — days more, perhaps, but still I could wait. Yes, the life of the world was a very long way away; after all, it did not matter.

How long I waited in this position I do not know, but it suddenly occurred to me that I was passing away, and for a moment all the old scenes came closer. They were passing by in a sort of procession.

A sudden impulse caused me to raise myself into a sitting position. I waved my hand above my head and shouted out, "Good-bye." The procession was over. I lay down again and waited for the end.

CHAPTER XX

AT THE MERCY OF THE HUN - AND AFTER

A BASIN OF SOUP
HOSPITAL AT ST. QUENTIN
THE "OPEN SESAME"

A MOMENT OR two later something occurred which caused my wearied brain to be roused again into activity. What could it mean?

I was again thinking hard, listening intently; something undefinable had happened to suddenly revive my mental condition. Had I passed away, and was this the next life? I felt like one who had awakened out of a dream in the dead of night, conscious that some one or something was moving near him.

"Englishman! Kamarade!"

Great God! I was found!

Had I the strength I should probably have screamed with joy, for that was my impulse at hearing a human voice. A second later and my feeling was to shrink from discovery. Surrender? Was it then to come to this, after all?

I did not answer; it was not necessary.

He must have heard me shout; he must know where I am. I was unarmed and helpless; what need to answer such a call? He would probably seek me, and I should be found without need to foul my lips with an answer.

And then I felt that it was not my life that was being saved, but a lingering death avoided by a murderous, but quick despatch. Well, perhaps it was better it should come that way.

Presently I heard some one crawling towards me. A few pebbles rolled down the slope, and there was silence again. I felt that he was looking down at me. Again a shuffle, and a quantity of loose earth rolled down the slope, and he was sliding down towards me.

The supreme moment had arrived. Would it be a bullet or a bayonet thrust; and where would it strike me?

I lay perfectly still. He seemed to be bending over me undecidedly. I thought he might believe me dead and go away without finishing me off, to seek the cause of the shout elsewhere.

I raised myself on my elbow and turned my face towards him. Then, to my astonishment he put his arms around my body and raised me up. What strange wonder was this? He put my arm around his neck, and with his own arm around my body, he raised me to my feet. But I could not stand. Then, placing both arms firmly around me, he dragged me out of the shell-holes. I felt myself being dragged several yards, and then he stopped.

I heard many voices talking below me. What would happen next. Then several hands caught hold of me, and I was lifted into a trench.

Some one gave an order, and I was dragged along the trench and around a corner. More voices seemed to come from still farther below. Some one picked hold of my feet, and I was carried down several steps. I was in a dugout.

It seemed warm and cosy. There were officers around me. Here must be the company commander whom I had driven away two days before. Now he could take his revenge. What mercy could I hope from him?

A voice asked me a question in English. But by this time I had collapsed completely. I tried to speak, but no sound would come from my throat. My head seemed to be an enormous size; my jaw would not move. I felt some one examine my tunic and examine my pockets. No, there were no papers there. I heard some one say "Hauptmann." Then more talking.

A cigarette was put in my mouth. I held it between my swollen lips, but could not inhale. A sharp command was given, and once more I was lifted up on to some one's back, and was being dragged down a long communication trench.

I was able presently to realise that I was in a dressing-station, for I was laid on a stretcher. Some one bent over me, evidently a medical officer.

My throat was parched. Oh, how thirsty I was! He was saying something to me in English in a very kindly manner. He opened a bottle of Seltzer water, and, lifting me up, placed it to my lips. Oh, how thirsty I was! I held out my hand for more. Bottle after bottle of Seltzer water was opened, and I drank one after the other. In my haziness I seemed to be wondering how they came to be supplied with such quantities of Seltzer water so close up to the front line.

He opened up my tunic and rubbed something on my chest. I heard him say, very gently:

"Injection against tetanus. It won't hurt you"; and then I felt a very slight pin prick. He laid me down again. My head was throbbing.

How hot and stuffy it was! I heard some groans, voices were speaking in a low tone. I again heard the word, "Hauptmann."

Of the days which followed I have only a hazy recollection. My brain and body sustained during the period of danger and strain, collapsed completely, and during the next six days I had only occasional periods of sensibility.

I can, therefore, only recall the facts between the time of my being picked up and my arrival at Hanover, six days later, in a disjointed manner.

Telling only of incidents, which stand out here and there in my memory, it must be borne in mind that during the operations of September the 8th and 9th I had felt the weight of my responsibility; and the great shock caused by my wound and the two days' exposure and suffering that followed, imposed a great strain upon my system, and reaction had now set in.

My wound had received no attention, and my right eye was hopelessly mutilated. The optic nerve of my left eye was damaged beyond repair, and the eye itself was obscured by an enormous swelling. My sense of smell was gone, and my cheeks, nose, and mouth were swollen and numbed to a painful degree.

I had lost power in my lower jaw, which would barely move. My nerves were completely shattered, and the mere touch of a hand would make me shrink with fright.

I had lost my voice, and during the occasional periods of sensibility, I could only speak in a startled whisper, while my brain in hideous delirium would constantly take me back to the scenes through which I had just passed.

I remember my stretcher being lifted and being placed in a horse-drawn ambulance with several others. Before leaving, the M. O. gave me a bottle of water, and so great was my thirst that for several days I kept this tightly gripped in my hand, and would not part with it except to get it refilled.

I have a hazy idea of being transferred from one ambulance to another, and several journeys.

The ground was very rough, and the shaking of the wagon seemed to cause great pain to other occupants. The bumping to my own head compelled me to raise it from the pillow and resist the jolts by resting it on my hand.

Where I spent Monday night I do not know, but on Tuesday night I found myself in what must have been a small hospital in a town I do not remember.

It seemed to me that I was in a sort of basement of a private house, and that a man and woman were watching over me, exhibiting very great kindness and compassion.

I seemed to awaken from my stupor, and remember some snatches of conversation, as they bent over me, for they could both speak a little English.

Blood and clay were still caked on my face and hair; and my uniform was sticky with blood and grime. Oh, how I wished I could take it off and be put into clean clothes and a bed!

The man was taking off my boots:

"Dese very goot boots, yah?"

I assented in a whisper.

"You have dem give you, yah?"

"No," I whispered, "bought them myself."

"Where do you buy such goot boots?"

"London."

"Ah, yah. I thought you would not get such goot boots for nothings. Look after dem well; we don't get goot boots like dat here."

I whispered to him:

"What is that noise?"

"Ah, it is a pity. Ze English zey have been firing ze long-range guns here, big guns. Zay carry twenty-seven miles. Ve moved dis hospital two times, yah."

The woman came up to my stretcher with a basin of soup. I shall never forget that basin of soup. It was probably very ordinary soup, but when I tasted the first spoonful I devoured it ravenously, for all this time I had not realised that I was suffering from starvation. For the past three days not an atom of food had passed my lips, and for two days previous to that an occasional bite of bread and cheese was my only ration. Even now I was not destined to receive the nourishment my body craved for; for one basin of soup per day was all I received during the remainder of that week.

Still grasping my bottle of water under my blanket, I was removed next morning and placed in a freight truck with two others —, one a sergeant in the Guards, and the other a private in the, London Regiment. We were locked in the truck, and kept there for many hours without food or conveniences of any kind, and finally arrived at St. Quentin.

Some one removed the blanket from my face and examined my shoulder-straps. I heard him say "Hauptmann," and after that I seemed to be treated with some consideration.

I did not understand a single word of German, and the repetition of this word puzzled me. It must have been some connection with my rank. I would try it on the next person who came near me and see what happened.

I had not long to wait, for by and by the stretchers were lifted and we were carried into the hospital at St. Quentin. I was placed alongside a large number of others, and the place created a very unpleasant impression of the attention I was likely to receive.

The place seemed like Bedlam. All round me I heard the groans and cries of the wounded. How long would I be left here unattended? How I longed to have my clothes removed! And what of my wound — how much longer must I go before it was attended to? And what was happening to it all this time?

I heard some voices near me speaking in German. Now was the time I would test that magic word, and see what would happen. Removing the blankets from my face, and lifting my arm to attract attention, I whispered hoarsely:

"Hauptmann!"

Some one stooped down over me, examined my shoulder-strap, and said, "Huhzo!" He then gave an order, and my stretcher was again picked up, and I was carried up-stairs to a room reserved for officers.

That "Open Sesame" served me in good stead on several occasions.

But the hospital at St. Quentin was a horrible place. There was a Frenchman in the ward who was raving mad, and between his yells and shrieks of laughter, the moaning of the wounded, and the fitful awakenings from my own delirium I spent a most unhappy time. I think I must have been there about two days, and on the morning after my arrival I was sensible for a while.

Adjoining the ward and only separated by an open doorway was the operating-room, where first operations were taking place hurriedly. The scene was something I can never forget. One by one we were being taken in, and the shrieks of pain which followed were too shocking for description. To hear strong men howl with pain is agonising enough; but to hear them shriek, and for those shrieks to fall upon the ears of nerve broken men awaiting their turn just outside the open door was terrifying, appalling.

As the shrieks subsided into weakened groans the stretcher would come back into the ward, and the next man be moved in; and so we waited in an agony of suspense, horror, and dread as nearer and nearer we came to our turn.

I do not wish to harrow my readers' feelings any more by describing how I felt when my stretcher was at last lifted and I was laid on the operating table. I could not see the bloodiness of my surroundings, but I murmured to myself, as I had occasion to do on subsequent and similar occasions:

"Thank God I'm blind."

There was a nurse at St. Quentin whose devotion and humanity will be long remembered by the many British and French wounded officers who have passed through that ward. In my half-dazed condition I seemed to have an idea that she was some sort of angel, whose gentle voice and comforting words were so soothing to the wounded, and inspired us with confidence in our painful conditions and surroundings.

On Friday, still greedily hugging my bottle of water, I was removed from St. Quentin and placed in a hospital-train bound for Hanover. I was told it was a splendidly appointed train, with every modern appliance.

The journey to Hanover occupied two days and two nights, but I remember nothing of it, as I believe I was unconscious the whole time.

I do remember just before leaving being presented with a haversack from the French Red Cross Society, and it was full of things which were extremely useful: a sleeping-shirt, handkerchiefs, biscuits, and similar articles. I have the haversack still. I carried it wherever I went in Germany, and never allowed it to leave my possession.

On Sunday morning, September 17, the train pulled into Hanover, and the wounded were carried out and left for a time on the platform.

Some girls seemed to be busy giving refreshment to the wounded. A girl came to my stretcher, pulled down the blanket which covered my face, and clumsily pushed the spout of a drinking-cup, containing coffee, into my mouth. I thought she was trying to feed me from some kind of teapot. The pot fell out of my mouth, and the coffee ran down my neck.

A man picked it up, and holding it to my lips, enabled me to sip it. I felt very grateful to him, for I was badly in need of sustenance. He spoke to me very kindly.

I thanked him in a whisper, and asked him if he was an officer.

He replied in English: "No, I am a waiter."

I think I became unconscious again. Rather unfortunate, for had I been stronger the humour of the remark would have amused me.

CHAPTER XXI
ALIVE

IT WAS THE first night after my arrival at Hanover that I really fully recovered a state of consciousness.

Although I have recorded several incidents of the week which had just passed, they were only occasional glimpses from which I would relapse again into unconsciousness, and it only comes back to me in a hazy sort of way, like dreams through a long night of sleep.

But I remember well the moment when I finally awoke and took in my surroundings. It was early in the morning. I seemed to have had frightful dreams; the horror of what I had passed through had been a frightful nightmare, mocking at me, laughing at me, blowing me to pieces.

I turned over on my side. Strange place this shell-hole; it seemed very comfortable. What was this I was touching — a pillow, bedclothes. Good God! I was in a bed! As my thoughts became clearer I lay perfectly still, almost in fear that any movement I might make would awaken me from this beautiful dream.

A long, long time ago something frightful had happened from which rescue was impossible. Yet, surely this was a bed.

Then I remembered the attack which had taken place over my body while I lay out in No Man's Land; of the shells which had burst around me in violent protest to my presence. I could not possibly have escaped; I must be maimed.

Cautiously I began to feel my limbs, my arms, my body, my feet, my fingers; they were all there, untouched. The whole truth dawned upon me: My God! I was alive!

I sat up in my bed; I wanted to shout and dance for joy. There was a bandage round my head: I was blind! Yes, I knew that, but there was nothing really the matter with me except that. The mere fact of being only blind seemed in comparison a luxury.

I was blind! But joy indescribable — what was that triviality — I was alive! alive!

Oh, my! I never knew before that life was so wonderful. Did other people understand what life was? No; you must be dead to understand what life was worth. I must tell every one how wonderful it all is.

But where was I? I could hear no guns — a bed? There were no beds at the front. I couldn't have dreamed it all; it must have been true; otherwise I should have been able to see.

Where then could I be? Oh, God! Yes, I know — I am a prisoner of war!

But even this knowledge, which for the moment quieted me, could not suppress my exaltation. I was saved! I was alive! No pain racked my limbs; no terror prodded my brain.

But I was weak and wasted. Oh, how weak I was! How hungry! But what of that, I was alive!

And where was England — such a long, long way off. I must go there at once, this minute. No, I can't; I'm a prisoner.

How miserable some people are who have no right to be. They cannot know how wonderful life is. Oh, how wonderful it is to die, and then to come to life again.

I'm only blind! Just imagine it! What is that? — it's nothing at all, compared with life; and when I get well and strong I won't be a blind man.

I may not recover my sight, but that doesn't matter a bit, I will laugh at it, defy it. I will carry on as usual; I will overcome it and live the life that has been given back to me.

I will be happy, happier than ever. I'm in a bed alive. Oh, God! I am grateful!

CHAPTER XXII
BLINDNESS

HOW RECKLESS WE are in referring to death! There are many people who would say they would prefer death to blindness; but the nearer the approach of death, the greater becomes the comparison between the finality of the one and the affliction of the other.

Those men, however, who have faced death in many frightful forms, and dodged it; suffered the horrors of its approach, yet cheated it; who have waited for its inevitable triumph, then slipped from its grasp; who have lived with it for days, parrying its thrust, evading its clutch; yet feeling the irresistible force of its power; men who have suffered these horrors and escaped without more than the loss of even the wonderful gift of sight, can afford to treat this affliction in a lesser degree, holding the sanctity of life as a thing precious and sacred beyond all things.

Even the loss of God's great gift of sight ceases to become a burden or affliction in comparison with the indescribable joy of life snatched from death.

There are men, and we know them by the score, who are constantly looking out on life through the darkened windows of a dissatisfied existence; whose conscience is an enemy to their own happiness; who look only on the dark side of life, made darker by their own disposition.

Such men, and you can pick them out by their looks and expression, who build an artificial wall of trouble, to shut out the natural paradise of existence; these men who juggle with the joy of life until they feel they would sooner be dead, do not know, and do not realise the meaning of the life and death with which they trifle.

Let us think only of the glory of life; not of the trivial penalties which may be demanded of us in payment, and which we are so apt to magnify until we wonder whether the great gift of life is really worth while.

Let us think not of our disadvantages, but of these great gifts which we are fortunate enough to possess; let us school ourselves to a high sense of gratitude for the gifts we possess, and even an affliction becomes easy to bear.

Here I am, thirty-six years of age, in the prime of health, strength, and energy, and suddenly struck blind!

And what are my feelings? Even such a seeming catastrophe does not appall me. I can no longer drive, run, or follow any of the vigorous sports, the love for which is so insistent in healthy manhood. I shall miss all these things, yet I am not depressed.

Am I not better off, after all, than he who was born blind? With the loss of my sight I have become imbued with the gift of appreciation. What is my inconvenience compared with the affliction of being sightless from birth.

For thirty-six years I had become accustomed to sights of the world, and now, though blind, I can walk in the garden in a sunny day; and my imagination can see it and take in the picture.

I can talk to my friends, knowing what they look like, and by their conversation read the expression on their faces. I can hear the traffic of a busy thoroughfare, and my mind will recognise the scene.

I can even go to the play; hear the jokes and listen to the songs and music, and understand what is going on without experiencing that feeling of mystery and wonder which must be the lot of him who has always been blind.

And the greatest gift of all, my sense of gratitude, that after passing through death, I am alive!

CHAPTER XXIII
THE WOMAN WHO WAITS

THE TELEGRAPH BOY'S RAT-TAT
KILLED IN ACTION
WEEKS OF MOURNING

MEANWHILE, WHAT WAS transpiring at home? What interpretation had been put upon my absence?

Many weeks later, after my first letter had reached home like a message from the dead, a post-card was handed to me from my father, which seemed to echo the sob of a broken heart. It was the first message to arrive from the England I loved so much, and my home, which I yearned for.

Letters from every member of my family were hastening towards me; but all were delayed except the single post-card, which told me only too plainly of the tragedy at home which was the result of my absence.

The message, written in a shaky hand, ran briefly, thus: "My son, for four weeks we have mourned you as dead; God bless you!"

In the despair of my heart my blindness and my bonds of captivity seemed to grow greater. In that simple message I realised the terrible truth, the full significance of the tragedy which had followed my fall.

What had been my suffering to theirs? After all I was a soldier, and mine was a duty. But those who wait at home — what of them?

The letters which followed confirmed my worst fears. I trembled and cried like a child.

How brave they had all been! How unworthy seemed my life to warrant the heroic fortitude and silent suffering which these letters unfolded! What were a few bullets compared with the pluck and silent self-sacrifice of the women of Britain, who were untrained to bear such shocks? What physical pain could compare with such anguish as theirs?

The first intimation reached my home by a letter returned from France, undelivered, and bearing a slip containing these words, typewritten: "Killed in action September 9."

Three days later a knock at the door, and a telegraph boy handed in a telegram which read:

"Most deeply regret inform you Cap. H. G. Nobbs — London Regiment, Killed in Action Sept. 9."

and also another telegram:

"The King & Queen deeply regret loss you and the Army have sustained by the death of Cap. Nobbs, in the service of his Country. Their Majesties deeply sympathise with you in your sorrow.
                                        "KEEPER OF THE PRIVY PURSE."

Next morning my name appeared in the official casualty list under the heading: "Killed in Action."

Letters followed from the front confirming my death, and even describing the manner of my death.

Such things are unavoidable in modern warfare; and only those who understand the conditions and the difficulties can appreciate the possibility of avoiding occasional errors. It is surprising to me that the errors in reporting casualties are not more frequent, and it speaks well of the care given by those responsible for this task.

It is extremely difficult, and occasional mistakes are only too apt to be widely advertised and give a wrong impression. Think of the task of the hundreds and thousands of casualties; and the errors, terrible though the suffering entailed may be, are comparatively insignificant.

But I have led the reader away from my story.

They thought me dead. Yes; killed in action. There was no getting away from it; no need for me to describe the tears and sorrow. Those who suffer must bear their sorrow in silence — more honour to them.

Obituary notices appeared in the newspapers, and letters and telegrams of condolence poured in.

My solicitors took possession of my belongings and explained their contents to my family.

A firm of photographers who generously invite officers to have their portraits taken free of charge, now offered the plate for a consideration to the illustrated papers; and even as I write these lines many months later, my picture is dished up again in this week's issue of an illustrated magazine as among the dead.

In short, during those few weeks which followed my fall, I became as dead and completely buried as modern conventions demanded.

It is expensive to die and not be dead, for clothes of mourning cannot afterwards be hidden under any other disguises; and it is a peculiar feeling to be called upon to pay for your own funeral expenses.

And when once you are officially dead it is very difficult to come officially to life again. Months have passed, and I am still waiting for the official correction to appear.

As I walk through the streets of London my friends stare at me as though I were a ghost. I feel as though I am a living apology for the mistake of others.

To the illustrated magazine I have just referred to I wrote assuring the editor that I had every reason to believe he was wrong in his contention. He replied, enclosing my photograph, and asking me if I was sure I was not some other person, as the picture referred to an officer who was surely dead.

Perhaps even now I am wrong. Yet, I ought to know.

CHAPTER XXIV
WARD 43, RESERVE LAZARETTE 5, HANOVER

OCCUPANTS OF THE WARD
CHIVALRY OF THE AIR

BEFORE THE WAR Reserve Lazarette 5 at Hanover was a military school. It is now used for wounded military prisoners, and for German soldiers suffering from venereal disease.

The same operating-room is used for all patients; the wounded prisoners receiving treatment in the morning, and the Germans in the afternoon.

There is a fair-sized garden, not unattractive, and the wounded are permitted to take the fresh air, and to walk about freely, if they are able to do so. So are the German patients, and so are their visitors, on Tuesdays and Saturdays, from 2 till 4 in the afternoon. There is no separation of the two classes of patients, and honour must share the company of disgrace in her captivity.

Ward 43 was a billiard-room in the old days, and the small-sized billiard-table is pushed against the wall and used as a table. There were nine beds in the ward; and four British and four French officers lay side by side in captivity.

The friendship of the two great nations was reflected in the maimed and pain-ridden bodies of these soldiers lying side by side, helpless, uncomplaining, but still champions of Anglo-French unity. Their cause is the same; their pain is the same; and side by side they lay, as side by side they had fallen.

Of the French officers I got to know but little, for they could speak no English, and the English could speak no French.

On my left was an officer of the Royal Flying Corps, Lieutenant

Donelly. He had been brought to earth after a fight thirteen thousand feet in the air, against five German planes. With his left arm disabled and three fingers shot off his right hand, and his engine out of action, he nose dived to the ground. A German aeroplane nose dived after him, all the while firing as it dropped.

With only a finger and thumb to manipulate his machine, he managed to effect a landing.

The moment earth was struck the firing ceased, and the Germans landing from their machines approached him and treated him courteously.

There is a spirit of chivalry among those who fight in the air, as both sides can testify. The air alone is their arena, and neither side will continue a combat on terra firma.

On my right was Lieutenant Rogan of the Royal Irish Regiment, a sturdy fellow, who had been in the Guards.

He was attacking some Germans, who were putting up a stout resistance during the fight for Guinchy; and as he was rushing forward, a German threw a hand-grenade, which exploded in his face. His right eye was removed at St. Quentin, and he was slowly recovering the sight of the left.

In the bed next to his was another young officer of the Royal Flying Corps, a boy about eighteen, very small, and only weighing about eight stone. Mabbitt was his name, Second Lieutenant Mabbitt; and he, too, had fought many thousand feet in the air against desperate odds, fracturing his leg in the fall.

German airmen seem to make a practice of waiting until a single English aeroplane appears in sight; then they ascend in a flight of five to attack, and woe betide the English airman who happens to be soaring above in a slow machine.

Deeds of pluck are common on land and sea; but the heroic combats in the air are a new sensation, with unknown terrors realised in a single gasp; and the youth of our country defy it. Yet, who is there to tell their deeds if they fall?

Shortly after I arrived two British officers were brought in, Lieutenant

Wishart of the Canadians, who had a bullet wound through his leg; and Second Lieutenant Parker, who had a hole in his leg as big as an apple, and who spent most of the day in declaring that he was as fit as a fiddle.

But the occupant of the remaining bed was one who endeared himself to the hearts of all. He was SANIEZ (pronounced Sanyea), our orderly. But Saniez must have a chapter to himself.

CHAPTER XXV
SANIEZ

RESERVE LAZARETTE 5, Hanover, boasted of no hospital nurses. There was no tender touch of a feminine hand to administer to the comfort and alleviate the distress of the wounded. There was no delicate and nourishing diet to strengthen the weak; neither did we expect it. We were prisoners of war, and though our sufferings were great, we were still soldiers.

But those who have passed through Ward 43 will always look back with gratitude and admiration on one whose unselfish devotion, tender care, and magnificent spirit was an example and inspiration to all of us.

His name was Saniez, the orderly in charge of the ward; a Florence Nightingale, whose unceasing attention day and night, whose tender watchfulness and devoted care and kindness made him loved and worshipped by the maimed and helpless prisoners who were placed under his charge.

Saniez was no ordinary man. No reward was his, except the heartfelt gratitude of those whom he tended. The wounded who passed through the ward left behind a debt of gratitude which could never be paid, and with a spirit of fortitude and courage created by his noble example.

There are compensations for all suffering; and no greater compensation could any wish for than the devotion of Saniez.

Saniez had suffered too, but would never speak of it. He had his moments of anguish and despair. He had a home, too; but his dreams he kept to himself, and his care he gave to others.

Saniez was a Frenchman, a big, burly artilleryman, with eyes bright, laughing, and sympathetic.

He had been captured nearly two years before; and suffered severely from the effects of frozen feet. Yet, painful as it must have been to get about, he seldom sat down.

All through those long days and nights weak voices would call him: it was always, "Saniez, Saniez!" and slop, slop, slop, we would hear him in his slippered feet, moving down the ward, attending to one and then another.

Saniez would be quiet and sympathetic, with a voice soft and soothing; and the next moment, cheerful and boisterous. Captivity could not subdue Saniez, or make him anything else than a loyal French soldier.

He would guard his patients against the clumsy touch of a German orderly like a tiger guarding its young. He would bribe or steal to obtain a little delicacy for his patients.

He seemed to know but a single German word, which he used on every possible occasion to express his disgust of the Germans. It was a slang word, but when Saniez used it, its single utterance was a volume of expression. It was nix, and when Saniez said nix, I knew he was shaking his woolly head in disgust.

Saniez had a marvellous voice, and when he sang he held us spellbound, and he knew it. I do not speak French, and could not understand his words, but his expression was wonderful; and he would fling his arms about in frantic gesticulation.

When Saniez sang he seemed to lift himself into a different atmosphere; he was back again in France; his songs all seemed about his country and his home. He seemed to rouse himself into a sudden spirit of defiance, and then his voice would grow soft and pathetic; and then slop, slop, slop, in his slippered feet, he would hurry off to a bedside to fix a bandage or administer a drink of water.

Every morning German soldiers could be heard marching past our windows, singing their national songs. We listened; Saniez would stop his work. What we wanted to say we would leave to Saniez, as broom in hand and eyes of fire he would wait until their voices died away in the distance, and then, with a fierce shake of his head he would shout: "Boche! Nix!" and, flinging his arms about his head, would sing the "Marseillaise."

One evening, and I remember it well, though no pen of mine can adequately describe the soul stirring picture — we had a concert in Ward 43. Four British and four French officers — a symbol of the Entente Cordiale — lay side by side in their cots, while convalescent prisoners from other wards sat in front to cheer them with song and music.

The Allies seemed well represented: An English Tommy with a guitar sang a comic song; a Russian soldier with a three-cornered string instrument, sang a folk-song of his native land; a Belgian soldier played the violin; and Saniez sang for France.

The applause that greeted the finish of each song was of a mixed kind; for those whose arms were maimed would shout, and those who could not shout would bang a chair or clap their hands. It was a patriotic and inspiring scene, and even the German orderly, coming in to see what was going on, was tempted to stop and listen.

We felt we were no longer prisoners; the spirit of the Allies was unconquerable.

Enthusiasm reached its highest pitch when Saniez brought it to a dramatic conclusion. Saniez had just finished a soul-inspiring song of his homeland. His audience could not withhold their applause until he finished, and Saniez could not restrain his spirit until the end of the applause. He suddenly threw up his arms, and at the top of his voice burst forth into the "Marseillaise," and the German orderly bolted out of the door.

Then the concert party ran to their dormitories; the lights were turned out, and we sought safety in sleep.

We used to ask Saniez about his home; and he seemed to grow quiet and confident. His home, he said, was about three miles behind the German line.

Some one suggested that it was in a dangerous place, as the British were advancing, and no house near the line could escape untouched; but Saniez was confident.

No! shells could not possibly harm it. His wife and sister lived there; it was his home. He was a prisoner, but whatever happened to him, the combined fury of the nations could not touch his home.

Saniez! Saniez! May you never awaken from your dream!

Captain Nobbs after his release from the German prison.

CHAPTER XXVI
LIFE IN HANOVER HOSPITAL

HOSPITAL DIET
INTERVIEWED BY A GERMAN DOCTOR
DISCHARGED FROM HOSPITAL

T HE DIET IN hospital can hardly be described as suitable for invalids. At the same time it was substantial as compared with what is received in prison camps. For breakfast we received coffee, with two very small, crusty rolls, each about the size of a tangerine orange; each roll cut in half, and a slight suspicion of jam placed between; for déjeuner one cup of coffee, one roll, and some very strong cheese, quite unfit to eat. The dinner was usually quite good, consisting of soup, a little meat and vegetables, and stewed apples or gooseberries. At 3 o'clock a cup of coffee and a small roll; at 6 o'clock supper, consisting of tea without milk, strong cheese, or German sausage or brawn, and a slice of bread.

For this diet we paid eighty marks per month.

An officer receives pay from the German Government on the following scale: lieutenant, sixty marks per month; captain, one hundred marks per month. The German Government recover the payments from the English Government, and it is charged against the officers' pay in England.

No food is supplied free to officers either in hospital or camp; and they cannot purchase anything beyond the regular issue.

With the exception of the dinner, I found the food of very little use to me for the first week or two, as having lost the power in my jaw, and being unable to open it more than half an inch, I couldn't tackle the rolls, and what couldn't be eaten had to be left; there was no substitute.

There was another diet, in which the coffee was replaced by hot milk, which would have been very desirable, except that the dinner consisted of some filthy substance, which was very unpalatable.

For the first week, therefore, I had practically only one meal a day, the dinner; but afterwards, by dint of changing from one diet to another I managed to get the dinner of No. 1 diet, and the milk of No. 2.

There was a canteen in the hospital where cigarettes, chocolates, biscuits, and eggs were offered for sale.

The biscuits were never in stock; the chocolate, though high in price, was so thin that there was nothing of it; and the cigarettes were unsmokable.

It was a sorry day when we could get no more eggs. We used to depend upon the eggs for supper; for the cheese was uneatable, the brawn suspicious, and the sausage like boiled linoleum. German sausage at the best of time is open to argument; but German sausage in a country which has been blockaded for two and a half years is worthy of serious thought.

The surgical attention was good, though the Russian prisoners who assisted were apt to be rough; and as neither the German doctor nor his Russian assistant could understand each other, and the wounded could understand neither, nor be understood in turn, the situation was sometimes difficult.

The doctor visited each bed at 8 A.M. every morning to inquire the condition of the wounded; but whatever you had to say — which of course he did not understand — the reply was always: "Goot, Goot."

On one occasion we saw flags flying over the city, and that evening for supper we were given a hard-boiled egg. We were told it was the Empress's birthday. We made anxious inquiries as to when the Kaiser and the Crown Prince would have a birthday.

A few days after I arrived at Hanover, my right eye was removed, and the following day the doctor told me, through an interpreter, that I should be sent back to England. I asked when I should be sent, and was told in three or four weeks.

It was about this time that I began to develop an insatiable appetite for sweet things. I have found that many have had the same experience, after a period of privation following upon their wounds. I would buy up all the jam, chocolate, and toffy I could lay my hands on, which came in parcels to other prisoners. When I wrote home for parcels to be sent to me, I hardly mentioned food, which afterwards became so necessary, but asked for sweet stuff.

But what I needed more urgently than anything else was money. When I was picked up the only cash I had on me was two francs, and this I exchanged for a mark and sixty pfennigs, which, with five marks I was able to borrow, kept me going for a while. But it was soon gone, and I found myself without a sou, and no pay due for six weeks.

About ten days after I arrived at Hanover I was able to sit out in the garden, and from then on I began to mend.

Saniez used to dress me, and his watchful eye was upon me wherever I went.

Sometimes of an afternoon I used to sit by the fire. I used to like sitting by the fire, because its warmth misled me into thinking I could distinguish the light. If I happened to be rather quiet Saniez would come to my side, and I would feel that he was watching me. Then he would speak, and each would find some word to make the other understand:

"Cigarette, Capitaine?"

"Oui, Saniez."

He would take one of his own cigarettes, put it in my mouth and light it.

I could neither taste nor smell it; but it pleased Saniez, so I took it.

"Très bien, Capitaine, puff, puff!"

"Oui, Saniez, très bien."

"Très bien, good. Monsieur Parker says, 'Trays beens.' Joke, ah, good joke!"

He would go away, but still watching me from a distance, would presently come back again, and placing his large hand on my shoulder, would say:

"Couche, Capitaine?" and leading me to my bed would lay me on it, and carefully tuck me in for the night.

There was a German non-commissioned officer employed in the hospital who was really a good sort. He could speak good English, having worked in English hotels before the war.

He would sometimes sit by my bed for a chat:

"Where were you wounded, Captain?" he asked one day.

"Leuze Wood on the Somme," I replied.

"Somme dreadful place, dreadful war, Captain."

"Very!"

"It is not fighting now; it is murder, both sides murder — yah."

"Have you been to the front yet?" "No; don't want to, either; don't like soldiering. German people sick of war; but got to do what we are told. Captain, you and I could settle it in five minutes."

"I'm not so sure; it's nearly settled me."

As the weeks passed by I began anxiously and earnestly to wait for news of my exchange; but three weeks went, and the fourth and fifth week passed, and still no news. About the seventh week Saniez burst into the ward one morning and rushed up to my bed.

"Bon jour, Capitaine. Good, good! Office, quick," and he began hurriedly dressing me.

I was to report to the office at once. I had been waiting for this, and dreaming of this moment for weeks.

Saniez knew it too, and as I went through the door I heard him shout:

"Angleterre, Capitaine; très bien!"

I waited outside the office for about half an hour. Wishart of the Canadians was inside, and presently he came out to fetch me:

"They want to see you inside. Who do you think is in there?"

"I don't know — who?"

"Doctor Pohlmann. He supervises all the prison camps belonging to the Tenth Army. We've got to go to a prisoners' camp."

My hopes were dashed to the ground.

He led me in, and I sat down before Doctor Pohlmann, who spoke excellent English, and explained that he was a doctor of languages.

He filled up a form, taking from me particulars of my name, regiment, and the usual details; and then, turning to Wishart, told him to go.

I began to feel that I was in for a rough time. Why did Doctor Pohlmann wish to speak to me alone.

I sat before him in silence, too disappointed at the turn events had taken to care what happened. But as soon as the door had closed he turned towards me, and his remarks surprised me beyond measure. Not a single question did he put to me to elicit information.

"Captain, you are quite blind?"

"Yes, quite."

"I am sorry; I did not know you were blind."

He seemed quite sympathetic. Not that I wanted it from him, yet so relieved was I to escape cross-examination that I felt quite bucked.

He continued: "The hospital people say you are ready to be sent away. When you leave here you come under my charge. They did not tell me you were blind. I have no proper place to put you; I do not know where to send you."

"If you will allow me, I can suggest a place."

"Ah, yes, I know, England. Of course you will be sent there in time, but in the meantime I must take charge of you. I will send you wherever you like. You can choose your own camp. What camp would you like to go to?"

"What camps have you got?"

"I have Gottisleau, Osnabruck, Blenhorst."

"Well, it's very good of you to give me the choice; but they all sound alike to me. How can I choose?"

"Have you any friends in either of them?"

"Well, really the names are unintelligible; I couldn't even repeat them. Lieutenant Rogan was sent away last week. Where did he go?"

"Ah, he went to Osnabruck. Good camp! Good commandant! I will send you and Wishart there, and I will arrange to put you three in one room together. If I can do anything for you at any time, let me know."

The interview was over. He was a plausible fellow, and he probably knew his job.

When I was getting ready to leave the hospital Saniez insisted on packing my clothes himself. I thought nothing about it at the time, but when I unpacked my clothes in camp I found concealed inside a small packet of sugar. Then I understood Saniez.

Wishart and I were told we could either walk to the station or pay for the hire of a motor-car. We rode to the station, laughing and talking, and smoking cigars which we obtained from the canteen.

CHAPTER XXVII
OBSERVATIONS AND IMPRESSIONS

EMPLOYMENT OF PRISONERS
PARCELS
MEN OF MONS

WHEN I FIRST became aware that there was a probability of my being exchanged I set to work to gather what information I could.

I came into contact with a good many private soldiers, and in conversation with them I became deeply interested in the commercial value of prisoners of war; for it appeared to me clearly evident that in a country where there were over a million prisoners, possibilities were unlimited; and the German authorities appeared, with businesslike organisation, to be taking the fullest advantage of their opportunities.

The unprecedented scale upon which prisoners have been made during the present war has opened up a problem unique in the annals of history. The more prisoners you take the more mouths you have to feed; and the greater becomes the man power necessary for their supervision.

With the ever-increasing number of prisoners the problem grows in enormity, and can either develop into embarrassing proportions, or by scientific handling can be turned to advantage.

In England for over two years we have herded our prisoners behind bayonets and barbed wire. The financial resources of the country have been poured out to feed idle hands, supplying food without repayment, at a time when the food and labour problems of the nation are becoming its most serious problems.

For over two years we have allowed the question to slide into obscurity, until to-day in our own country the only part of the community which has no anxiety or participation in the problem of living and daily sustenance is the German prisoner in our midst; and yet to-day a large part of what should be our fighting power is kept from the firing-line to supply the needs of the nation and feed the mouths of our idle prisoners.

It has never occurred to us, or if it has we have ignored it, that without contravening the law of nations, prisoners can be made to feed themselves, and be employed in any industry, provided they are not put to work connected with the war.

It has never occurred to us that we have in our midst many of the trade secrets of a country which for generations has been our rival in commerce.

It has never occurred to us that Germany has in her midst men who hold the trade secrets of our empire, and is learning them day by day by the employment of our men in her industries.

If we neglect this problem any longer we may find that when the world resumes its normal trade activity Germany, on this point at any rate, will have scored a commercial victory.

The nations of the world are at war. But the armies of to-day are civilian armies, comprising men of industrial and commercial education, and the prisoners of to-day are men of commercial and industrial value.

Our adversaries have been quick to recognise this. We seem to be still imbued with the idea that the German soldier in our midst is simply a fighting machine!

So he is. But when the time came for the civilian to take up arms and supplement the professional fighting force, there fell into our hands an industrial fighting machine in the guise of a military prisoner.

We have the impression that a military prisoner is an individual whose one desire is to escape and jump at our throats; and that the safety of the nation compels us to stand over him with a bayonet and regard his every movement with suspicion.

Yes, I do not deny that a very large number of prisoners in our midst would be glad to get back to their homeland, especially if there was no further prospect of having to face the British in the firing-line. But keep a man idle for months behind barbed wire, like an animal in a cage, and you encourage his desire to escape far more than if you diverted his mind by industrial employment.

Have we not a barbed wire supplied by nature completely surrounding our country? Are we not on an island?

I had many opportunities of talking with our men in Germany and of gaining information as to the manner in which the German authorities were taking advantage of the problem we avoid, or occupy our time in idle discussion.

I will take one concrete example. In Hameln Lager the commandant has charge of 50,000 prisoners, of which 30,000 are "living out!" They are working out in commandos on the farms, in the factories, in the workshops; in large batches, small batches, and even singly.

I met one man who had been employed alone in a wheelwright's shop. He was a wheelwright by trade. How many wheelwrights' shops are there in England which could do to-day with one of the wheelwrights we are keeping idle behind barbed wire?

What information did that man's employer gain by the way the work was done? How simple the method of obtaining the labour: simply go to the labour bureau attached to the imprisonment camp nearest to your workshop, and ask for a wheelwright. You keep your industry going, and thus in the only practical way keep open the job for the man who is called to the colours.

The employer pays the man no wages, but the local trade-union rate of wage is paid to the commandant who supplies him. Thirty thousand prisoners from a single camp contributing to the industry of the nation, and the wages of 30,000 prisoners contributing to the cost of the war. The prisoner receives through the commandant 30 pfennigs (3d.) per day, and is glad of the employment.

A very large number of prisoners are employed as agricultural labourers, and it is quite reasonable to suppose that all the food supplied to the prisoners, such as it is, is grown by prisoner labour.

I was told by men who had worked on farms that they were compelled to work from 4 in the morning until 9 at night. In some cases only one or two were employed on small farms.

I asked those men why they did not embrace the opportunity to make their escape. But they said that while the work was hard they preferred it; as they lived with the farmer, who treated them well if they worked well. They ate at the farmer's table, and had no non-commissioned officers to bully them; whereas, if they attempted to escape and were caught they would be sent to work in the mines or other equally unpopular task.

Large numbers are employed in the sugar-refineries, coal-mines, and salt-mines, the latter task being the most dreaded; for with the food they were given their health broke down within a few months.

The English prisoner said that when the party he was with first arrived at the mine and saw what they had to do they refused to work. Their guard thereupon threatened them, and when they still refused they were taken outside one by one, and the remainder would hear a shot fired, and then another would be taken out.

It was a fake. The men could not be intimidated, and they were sent back to the Lager.

It was on another occasion that the man I am referring to was put to work in the mine.

I was asked by another if I knew anything about 200 German prisoners being sent back to work in France, because they were not allowed to work in England. He said that when the Germans heard about it they took 200 of our men from Doberitz camp and sent them to work in Poland as a reprisal.

The work there may not have been very much harder, but it was a great hardship upon our men, because there would be a considerable delay in their parcels of food reaching them from England, and meantime they had to subsist on the scanty fare supplied by their captors.

The men seemed to be getting parcels on a very liberal scale. Some were getting more than others, but they divided up by eating in messes of four or six, or some such number.

I did not hear of many complaints of parcels being undelivered, though in some cases parcels were missed. But so far as I could ascertain they were not withheld in any deliberate or systematic manner; and when one comes to consider the enormous number handled and the probability of parcels getting lost through insecure packing, the number of complaints I heard of seemed comparatively insignificant.

The Russian prisoners seemed to be the least provided for, and parcels for them were very rare. They lived or rather starved on the German rations; and when men have to work or remain in the open air all day such a ration was a form of torture.

When the watery liquid of potato water called soup was issued from the kitchens fatigue parties were paraded to draw the issue for each mess.

The British prisoners were not altogether dependent on this ration, and would let the Russian prisoners carry the dixy for them, and in return they would be given a cup of soup by the British Tommies. So hungry were the Russians for this little "extra" that hundreds of them would wait for hours in the cold on the off-chance of a few getting the job.

One cannot speak with these British Tommies and hear of their hardships without feeling a profound admiration for their indomitable spirit. You can take a British soldier prisoner, send him far from the protection of his country, but he is British wherever he goes and his courage and resourcefulness cannot be broken.

Whenever I met a man who had been a prisoner since the beginning of the war, I made a point of getting his story to ascertain the truth about the barbarities I had read of.

There was no mistaking these men. I could not see them but I seemed instinctively to recognise, and whether it was my imagination or not I cannot tell; but their manner seemed distinctive and they spoke like men who had suffered much and were harbouring a just grievance, and lived for the day when they would revenge themselves. As one man put it to me:

"If we ever see a German in England when we get back we will kill him."

These men were taken at Mons; captured, most of them, by sacrificing themselves in rear-guard fighting to save the main British army.

These men have been in captivity for two and a half years. Just think of it! But do we think of it enough, or have we forgotten it?

The British Tommy has an individuality which is not always understood. Ask him in an official way to give evidence of his treatment, and he will sit tight and say not a word. Take out your notebook to write down his evidence and he can think of nothing, but all the same he knows a lot.

I know this to be true; for after I was exchanged I spoke to a soldier who had been exchanged at the same time, and he said that a Government official had been round to question the men on the treatment they had received in Germany. During our conversation he told me that 200 of our men had been put to work in a Zeppelin factory. I asked him if he had given this in evidence, but he said:

"No, not likely; they got nothing out of me."

I asked him why not, for it was his duty. But he said they would only have asked him a lot more questions to try and tie him up in a knot.

When I came across a soldier who was captured at the beginning of the war I used to invite him to my room when no one was about. We would sit in front of the fire and drink a cup of cocoa and smoke a pipe.

I never asked him questions, but let him talk as he felt like it. There were generally one or two others in the room, and when we began to feel we knew each other and were chums together in adversity, he would tell his story in his own way.

I met these men in Hanover Hospital, Osnabruck camp, and Blenhorst camp. I will not publish their names for fear of paining their relatives; but I have their names and the names of witnesses who heard the stories, which I will relate in my next chapter.

CHAPTER XXVIII
STORIES OF THE HEROES OF MONS

THE STATEMENTS WHICH follow, and which were made to me while I was a prisoner of war in Germany, are not from picked soldiers who happened to have sensational stories. They were the only men whom I met who were prisoners in the early days.

Being blind myself, I could not, of course, see the men I was speaking to, but their tone impressed me very much as being men who had suffered in silence.

It was necessary for me to study very carefully what they said and impress it on my memory; and I have committed their statements to writing immediately on my release, for to carry written statements over the frontier was entirely out of the question.

I have put down nothing which was not told to me; neither have I tried to embellish or enlarge upon the statements made, or frame the words of the men in any way that might give an exaggerated impression of what occurred.

It is quite possible, however, that one or two incidents which I have reported from one man may be part of the story of one of the others. But it can be taken as an absolute fact that, taken as a whole, the statements are a true recital of these men's own description of their experience.

The men were in no way excited. I obtained the information when chatting in the ordinary way over a pipe of tobacco, whenever the men had an opportunity of coming to my room to have a chat.

THE STORY OF PRIVATE —— , WEST KENT REGIMENT

"I was captured at Mons, sir. Been here over two years now. Things are not so bad now as they were at first.

"I've seen some things which I shan't easily forget. I've been keeping them to myself because we dare not talk of them."

"Some of the fellows have had a terrible time. When the war is over any German who is met in England by any prisoners of war will have a rough passage. There won't be any need to hold ourselves back any longer. My goodness, sir, they'll never get away alive!

"Not long after I was captured 70 English soldiers were taken away from the Lager one day. They never knew where they were going. They were taken to a munition factory; and when they found out where they were they passed the word along to refuse to work.

"When the Germans told them what they had to do, they refused. Their guards threatened them, and said it would be the worse for them if they didn't; but they wouldn't budge.

"Then they were taken out and made to stand in a row against a wall; and a firing-party was drawn up in front of them with loaded rifles, but not one of them flinched.

"They were told that unless they went to work they would be shot, and although the firing party was standing in front of them not one of them would budge.

"The threat was not carried out, and they were sent back to the Lager.

"Before we started getting parcels we had a terrible time trying to live on the food they gave us. All they gave us was a cup of coffee and two slices of black bread in the morning; and for dinner and supper a basin of hot potato water. It was so thin and weak it was just like water that potatoes had been boiled in."

The soldier whose statement is given above has since been exchanged to Switzerland, owing to an injury to his sight, caused by the work he was employed upon while a prisoner.

THE STORY OF PRIVATE —— OF THE LEICESTER REGIMENT

"I was captured during the retreat in August, 1914.

"My Company was left behind as a rear-guard, to enable the rest of the battalion to get away. Our trench was only about two feet deep. Although the Germans were coming on very fast and in enormous numbers, we were not allowed to retire.

"The Germans charged us three times. We lost all our officers, and although we kept on fighting they came on in such large numbers it must have been the main body, for they were all round us, and most of the fellows were killed or wounded.

"They had their revenge on us, too, when they got us, for the German soldiers who were told to look after us did terrible things. They took us one by one and made us run the gauntlet.

"I was bruised all over when I got through, and so were the other fellows.

"One chap when he was running the gauntlet was struck in the face by the butt of a rifle; his nose was smashed and his face covered in blood, and he fell to the ground insensible. They threw him in a ditch, because they thought he was dead; but he was able to crawl out next morning.

"It was awful, that first night, and they didn't know what to do with us. They made us stand the whole night through in a loose wire entanglement, so that we couldn't walk about or sit down; and it rained like anything all night long.

"Then we were put in cattle trucks and sent into Germany, and for the first two days they did not give us any food or water.

"On the second day we stopped at a station and a woman came towards us with a large can of soup, and we thought we were going to be fed; but she brought it right up to us, and said: 'Ugh, dirty Englanders,' and poured it on to the line.

"I was taken to Soltau Lager; and the food they gave us consisted of a cup of acorn coffee in the morning and a small piece of black bread, which had to last all day, and wouldn't make more than two good slices.

"For dinner we got a basin of very thin potato soup; sometimes we got a potato in it, and sometimes we didn't. For supper we got a cup of coffee, and we were supposed to make the bread do for both breakfast and supper.

"The prisoners were sent out from Soltau in working parties to farmers, factories, and coal mines and salt mines. The salt mines were dreaded most, and fellows who had been working there for two or three months looked dreadful. In fact, they could not keep up there longer than that; they got too ill.

"I was sent into a salt mine myself. The hours are not long, because it is impossible to stay down many hours at a time, and we were generally brought up about one o'clock. They did not keep me in the mine long, because they found I was of no use for the work.

"It's not so bad on the farms, although you have to work from about 4 o'clock till 8 or 9 at night. But the food is better, as you generally live at the farmer's table, and have the same as he does.

"When prisoners are sent in working parties, the employers have to pay the German Government the same wages he usually pays a man, and the prisoners receive from the German Government 30 pfennings (about 3d.) per day."

"Did the American Consul ever visit the lagar?" I asked.

"Yes, but only once when I was there."

"Were you free to make any complaints to him if you wished?"

"Two of the fellows did; but they got punished for it.

"Before he visited the lager a notice was put up that the Commandant did not consider there was any reason for complaint, and any man making a complaint would be given 14 days' imprisonment.

"When he called we were drawn up on parade in four companies, and stood to attention, while he passed down the line, asking if there were any complaints.

"By his side was the Commandant and another German officer."

THE STORY OF PRIVATE —— OF THE NORFOLK REGIMENT

"I came out with the original Expeditionary Force, and was in the retreat from Mons, but was not captured until October, 1914.

"The German soldiers who captured me treated me quite well. They gave me some of their rations, and allowed me to attend to our wounded.

"I had just bandaged up the leg of a man in the Cheshire Regiment, who had half his foot blown off, when all the prisoners were ordered to the rear.

"A German officer came up and ordered us both to get back; but I pointed out that the Cheshire man was too badly wounded to be moved without help. He ordered me to undo the bandage, and when he saw the condition of the wound, he drew his revolver and shot him dead. He then ordered me to get back.

"We were then sent into Germany, and when we stopped at the Railway Stations school children were paraded on the platform and threw things at us.

"We were given nothing to eat, and at one station we appealed to a clergyman, who spoke English; but he said that only German soldiers should be fed, and turned away.

"I was sent to Hameln Lager. I was several times sent out with working parties, and we were sometimes treated very roughly, especially when there was only an under officer in charge of us.

"The job I liked best was working for a farmer. Sometimes you get hold of a decent chap, who will treat you well, if you suit him. The work is hard and the hours very long, but you live with the family, and food is much better than what you get in camp; especially as some of the farmers have food concealed.

"The under officers are very rough, and stop at nothing.

"There was a notice up in the lager which said that no man has any right to refuse to work, and that only the laws of the Imperial German Government were recognised; and if any man refused to do what he was told, the guards had authority to use their rifles."

"Did they ever use them?" I asked.

"I never saw them myself; but a man came into the lager one day who said that just before he was moved one of the men was being badgered about by his guards, until he at last turned round and knocked one down. The guards immediately ran their bayonets into him, and he died next day.

"The American Consul visited our camp shortly afterwards, and this man told him about it, and was informed the matter was already known, and was being investigated. I do not know if anything came of it.

"Another little trick which they used to employ to force men to work in the mines and other places was to take them out one by one under an armed guard. The rest of us would hear a shot fired, and then they would take another; a shot would be fired, and so on. But we soon got on to that, because we found it was a fake.

"About 100 men were taken away from the lager in the early part of the war to work in a factory, but when they found it was a munition factory they refused to work. They were each sentenced to twelve or fifteen months' imprisonment. I know this for a fact, because I have spoken to the men. They were very badly treated, and one of them is in hospital to-day, insane."

The Story of Private —— of the Middlesex Regiment, Told Me in Blenhurst Camp

"I was at Soltau Lager for a long time before we came here. We used to get one loaf of black bread a day (2 lbs.) between 10 men. The only food we got was some sort of coffee for breakfast, and the same for supper. For dinner we had a basin of soup, which was almost undrinkable, some thin washy stuff; occasionally we got some potatoes.

"In the early part of the war there were about 60 of our fellows sent to work in a munition factory. But when they got there and saw what they had to do, they refused. They were threatened with all kinds of things to make them work, and then they were lined up against a wall, and a number of German soldiers stood in front of them, and told them that if they didn't work, they would be shot. Then they made a show of loading, and brought their rifles up to the shoulders. When our men still refused they were taken into a building and locked up two or three in a room; and left there for 3 or 4 days without food or water or convenience of any kind."

I asked Private —— if he was quite sure of this statement and the length of time, as the men would be reduced to a state of absolute starvation.

"I am quite sure about it," he said, "and as for the men being starved, I can only tell you that they were found curled up on the floor, gnawing at their finger-nails."

"When the Commandant let them out he said he was going to send them back to their lager, as he admired their pluck, and didn't think Englishmen had so much in them."

CHAPTER XXIX

OSNABRUCK

ARRIVAL IN CAMP
THE CANTEEN
DAILY ROUTINE
RATIONS
PARCELS
NEWS

W E LOOKED FORWARD to the journey with a great deal of pleasure, not that I could see where I was going, but the sensation of travelling was a pleasant change.

We had about half an hour to wait for our train at the station, to the intense interest of a crowd of 60 or 70 peasants, who gathered around us and gazed in open-mouthed wonder.

As a matter of fact I was quite unaware that we were the centre of attraction. I thought we were standing quite alone. It is not a disadvantage to be blind sometimes.

We had a guard with us of one soldier with a revolver in his belt, which no doubt was fully loaded, though we did not trouble him to prove it.

We were placed in a very comfortable second class carriage, quite equal to an English first-class carriage. German officers also appear to travel second class; and on all the journeys I made in Germany, I was always treated on an equality in this respect.

Half-way through the journey we had to change, and had to wait about three-quarters of an hour for a connection. We were glad of this, as we were looking forward to a meal in the station restaurant. But we were doomed to disappointment. On entering the restaurant there were plenty of tables and chairs, but to all appearances nothing to eat.

We sat down at a table in company with our escort, and Wishart went over to the counter to order a hot meal, but could not make himself understood. After energetically ordering every dish he could think of, including eggs and bacon, and emphasising his wishes by violent gesticulations, he returned unhappily to the table and sought the assistance of the guard, who was made to understand that in England the object of entering a restaurant is for the purpose of getting something to eat.

We were finally provided with a cup of coffee, a piece of cheese, and a slice of very stale and uninteresting bread.

We arrived at Osnabruck station at about 9 P.M., and were placed in a four-wheel cab, our guards sitting opposite us, with another soldier, who met us at the station, sitting on the box seat, thus attracting the attention of the passersby and conjecture as to the distinguished occupants of the cab, whose cigars by this time were unfortunately exhausted.

We had a drive of about four miles, for Osnabruck camp is situated on the outskirts of the town; and we were greeted on arrival by a request from the cabby for ten marks.

After having been in daily expectation of a voyage to England, my arrival at Osnabruck camp gave me a fit of the blues; and I felt like one who enters a prison to undergo a term of penal servitude.

We knocked at the outer gate, which was securely locked, and were challenged by a sentry, who was answered by our guard. There was really no need to challenge us, for as far as Wishart and I were concerned, we were perfectly willing to remain outside the domain of his authority.

We heard a clatter of rifles, as the guard was turned out to welcome our visit, and after an examination of our papers to make sure that we had the right to enter, we were marched across the courtyard and stopped before a very large door. More knocking and a noise as of bolts being drawn back, and we entered the building.

As the door was closed and bolted behind me, I felt like one who was losing his freedom for ever in the dungeons of a mighty fortress.

We were led into the canteen, and the canteen manager supplied us with a cup of tea and a slice of bread and margarine — the margarine being a rare luxury for a prison camp.

We were next taken into an office and searched and our money exchanged for canteen money. This precaution is always taken, so that if a prisoner escapes he is not likely to have any negotiable money upon him.

I thought the soldiers who searched us were very fair, for seeing I was blind, they allowed Wishart to see exactly the money I had upon me, so that there could be no dispute. As a matter of fact I handed out the money myself.

They did not search me, but asked me if I had anything on me which should be given up, and now I come to think of it, although others were always rigorously searched, I do not ever remember having been searched myself. They always took my word for it; perhaps it was because I was blind and they thought I was harmless.

We were then taken up to a room on the second floor. Doctor Pohlmann was as good as his word, and a room for three was provided, Rogan being in possession.

Osnabruck camp is part of a cavalry barracks, and the accommodation, therefore, is what one would expect in English barracks, and quite suitable for soldiers.

The rooms are comfortable; there is a small stove with coal provided, and the furniture consists of camp-beds with two blankets each, a chest of drawers and a small table and chair. Some of the rooms contain as many as seven beds, but the rooms are fairly large and do not appear to be overcrowded.

Doctor Pohlmann told us that the camp boasted, among other attractions, a billiard-room. Probably he was right, but he must have forgotten to add that there was no billiard-table or other article of furniture in it.

A large room was set aside for the British prisoners, and another for the Russian prisoners; these were furnished at the prisoners' expense with a piano and card-tables, and used as anterooms. The British anteroom, however, never seemed popular, as the officers preferred their own living rooms, which were warmer.

The French had no anteroom, although I think they could have secured one had they desired it.

There were about 250 prisoners in the building, about 200 of whom were Russian and French.

There was a canteen, where almost everything but food could be obtained. The beer was not bad, and fairly cheap; but the only other drinks obtainable were a yellow fluid and a reddish fluid, which was given by the canteen manager the humorous description of sherry and port wine.

He was a wise man, that canteen manager, for under what strategical device could he have extracted one mark per glass from his customers, and at the same time supply a "have another" atmosphere to his establishment? But he was a good fellow, and added greatly to the comfort of the officers (and to the comfort of his own banking account).

You could buy anything from him (except food), from a toothpick (which he never caused us to need) to a grand piano (which he did not keep in stock).

He would purchase on commission, and the latter part of the purchase he gave particular attention to. But he sought custom, and it made him civil and obliging. He would supply you with a kettle of boiling water for 5 pfennigs; or, for a larger consideration, would cook the pheasant which came in your last parcel.

The grounds outside the building were very small, although just before I left a field was thrown open, where the officers could kick a ball about. There were also two tennis-courts built by the officers.

The picture does not seem an unpleasant one; and I do not think the officers imprisoned there ever complain of their treatment. But if it were a marble palace, that would not alter the fact that it was a prisoners' camp; and two hours was about as long as anybody would stay without being bored.

If the description I have given leaves the impression that the prisoners have a good time in such seclusion, a stroll around the building a few times, avoiding the barbed wire; or a few nights' sleep disturbed by the frequent challenge of the sentry and the barking of the watch-dogs would disillusion them, and make them realise what it means to feel the strong fetters of captivity.

In England we treat German officers very liberally; and if we ever allow this to arouse our indignation, we should pause to remember that this generous treatment has induced the German authorities to grant favours to British officers.

Our officers, for instance, on signing a parole, are allowed once or twice each week to go for a long country walk in company with only one German officer; and this privilege is at any rate worth an equal amount of consideration being shown towards the German officers in England.

A medical officer is present each morning, and if it is necessary to attend hospital, or the dentist, or if you have permission to go down for any other purpose, you are allowed the privilege of hiring a conveyance for what the cabby probably flatters himself is a moderate charge; but if you do not wish to pay for this privilege, you can walk — in the gutter.

The dentist was not a popular man to visit, although a prisoner is often tempted to sacrifice a tooth in order to enjoy the privilege of a ride down-town. But he was apt to use his professional skill as an instrument to his patriotic ardour, and appeared to aspire to the removal of the jaw instead of the tooth.

During the time I was at Osnabruck, there was a good commandant in charge. He was a gentleman, fair-minded, and considerate, notwithstanding the fact that he was a professional soldier of the old school.

When I speak of the old school, it leads me to express an opinion that the brutalities perpetrated upon our soldiers who fell into their hands in the early part of the war were due to professional military hatred more than to popular intention. At the commencement of the war, the professional German soldier seemed to be imbued with the sole idea, which was no doubt fostered by the system of training, to get to England, and satisfy his hunger by murder and pillage; and the first prisoners who saved the people of this country by their heroic self-sacrifice received the first experience of their intentions.

My contention is borne out by the fact that these brutalities are not practised to-day in anything like the same degree, for the old army has become more or less extinct, and a new army of civilians has taken its place. With the exception, perhaps, of certain elements of the higher commands, there is a decreasing element of the "top dog" spirit, and an undercurrent of feeling that it may not be wise to be too overbearing.

To-day it is the German civilian fighting the British civilian, and the German who has a home, family, and business has not the same hatred as his professional predecessor.

The German professional soldier is unapproachable; but the German civilian soldiers seemed reasonable and anxious for peace, and even to deplore the domineering authority which compelled him to take up arms.

At Osnabruck the roll-call was made by the officers simply parading outside of their respective rooms and coming to the salute as the German officer passed him, and he, in passing by, would answer the salute. The morning roll-call was at 9 A.M., so at one minute to nine it was necessary to tumble out of bed.

The curious raiment frequently donned more with a view to speed than dignity prompted an order being issued that officers should parade fully dressed. The ingenuity of the British soldier, however, could soon overcome a requirement of this kind. One minute to nine still prevailed, but the wearing of overcoats for early morning roll-call grew in popularity.

I was very much impressed with the fair and systematic handling of our parcels, letters, and money; and even letters and post-cards which arrived for me after I had been sent back to England were readdressed and sent back. A remittance of five pounds, which arrived for me after I had left was even returned to me in England, instead of being applied to the pressing need of the German War Loan.

Letters are distributed each morning. Parcels arrive on Mondays and Thursdays, and a list is made out and sent round the same afternoon, from which each prisoner can ascertain the number of parcels awaiting him. He thereupon appears at an appointed hour the following day to receive his parcels, which are opened by the German censor in his presence.

All tin food has to be opened, but if it is not required for immediate consumption, it is placed unopened in a locker, and he can draw what he requires on any day he wishes to use it.

The American Express Company was permitted to cash officers' cheques through the paymaster, who kept a proper account of the debits and credits against each prisoner; so that he could draw money at any time from the funds standing to his credit. These accounts were kept in a very businesslike manner, and a prisoner was permitted to go into the paymaster's office and examine his books whenever he wished. I know of at least one instance in which a prisoner had been permitted to overdraw his account.

The prisoners spent most of their time at Osnabruck in playing tennis, football, walking up and down the yard, learning French or Russian, playing cards, or reading.

The books which prisoners receive from time to time from England are passed round, thus forming a sort of circulating library.

In living a life of this kind one cannot help but develop the habits of school-days, and become boyish in many things.

One lives for letters and parcels. It is not the length of letters or size of parcels which count so much as the number; and when the parcel list comes round, he is a lucky fellow who finds four or five parcels awaiting him, even though their total contents amount to no more than that of the man who receives a single parcel.

On Tuesdays and Fridays the number of parcels was an absorbing topic, and one would turn to another in schoolboy fashion, and say:

"How many parcels have you got to-day?"

"Only one — how many have you?"

"Six."

"Lucky devil!"

In each room the men throw their parcels into one mess, and share alike; and if a new prisoner arrives, who would not be receiving parcels, he shares with the others in his room.

If several prisoners just arriving are put in a room by themselves, they do not, of course, fare so well, and until their parcels arrive, many weeks later, they are more or less dependent upon the food issued to them; although presents of food are frequently sent in by the others, and articles of clothing are loaned.

The charge made to the prisoners for food was forty-five marks per month. We were afterwards informed that by a new regulation the charge, by some international arrangement, had to be reduced to thirty marks per month. And the commandant explained that for this sum he could only supply the same ration which the men received; but would continue to supply the old ration if the officers would voluntarily agree to continue paying forty-five marks, and extra for their bread — which, of course, they did.

This ration consisted of imitation coffee for breakfast and no food. A plate of washy stuff called soup, for dinner, followed by some sloppy mashed potatoes, and sometimes green stuff; and for supper, more sloppy potatoes.

To satisfy one's hunger on a cold day with such food — which is only fit for pigs — can only be done by loosening the waistcoat, and half an hour afterwards one feels as though he had never had a meal.

Prisoners were allowed to receive as many letters as they were lucky enough to have sent them; and there does not appear to be any restriction as to the length of the letter.

They are allowed to write two letters of four pages each, and four post -cards each month. All letters are censored by a staff of censors in the camp. Outgoing letters and post-cards are held for ten days, with a view of ascertaining, I believe, whether invisible ink had been used.

News arrives in the camp principally by the arrival of new prisoners, who are kept in quarantine for about ten days.

German official bulletins are posted in the anteroom; and the *Continental News*, which is published in the English language, or rather disgraces the English language by using it, is delivered daily. By the bye, the *Continental News* is a rag of the worst kind, and contains lies of the worst description.

My orderly came to me one day, and after carefully closing the door, he drew from under his tunic a few scraps of an English newspaper a month old.

We devoured the news eagerly, as well as the advertisements, and passed it quietly around to the other officers.

He had been sweeping up the canteen after the censor had finished opening up the parcels. One parcel had been wrapped up in the newspaper, and unthinkingly the censor overlooked it, and tore the paper into fragments and threw it on the floor.

My orderly, while sweeping, noticed the pieces on the floor. The censor was in the room, and he went on sweeping until, when the censor's head was turned, he stooped and, snatching it up, stuffed it into his tunic.

CHAPTER XXX
COMEDY AND DRAMA

I SALUTE THE WALL
THE STORY OF AN EGG
A NOVEL BANQUET
JOY RIDE ON A LORRY
THE SWISS COMMISSION

WHEN I ARRIVED at Osnabruck, I found three English orderlies, and to my surprise and delight, two were men of my own regiment who had been captured at Gommecourt Wood on July 1st.

The commandant came up to visit me the following morning, something very unusual; but no blind prisoner had ever been confined within the walls of Osnabruck before, and I suppose I was an object of interest.

I heard Rogan say, "Commandant," and click his heels.

I stood up and saluted. I was turned around, for, unknowingly, I had gravely saluted the wall.

He spoke fairly good English:

"You quite blind?"

"Yes, quite."

"See no light — nothing, no?"

"Nothing whatever."

"Your health, vot, is your health goot — yah?"

"Very weak and shaky; I cannot sleep at night."

"Is there anything you want?"

"There are two orderlies here from my own regiment. Can I have one as my personal attendant? Otherwise I am helpless; I am not yet accustomed to blindness, and among so many people and in strange surroundings, I shall become a nuisance."

"Yah; I will make arrangements."

That was how I came to get Private Cotton as my orderly. Cotton was a fine lad; a well educated, superior type of fellow, and we became very much attached to each other during those long, dreary days.

He could speak French, and although he could speak no German, he possessed that wonderful faculty peculiar to the private soldier, of understanding and making himself understood in a language he did not know.

He had been a civil servant in the War Office; but in the early part of the war had volunteered his services with the colours, and fought night and day in the trenches for a shilling a day; while the young man who took his place in the War Office drew one and sixpence an hour overtime after 4 o'clock. Yet Cotton never complained. But his duty was the other man's opportunity.

As I write these lines Cotton is still a prisoner. I wonder if the other man is still drawing overtime, and wearing a war-service badge?

Now Cotton was a gentleman both by birth and education; but he was a private soldier, and seemed to make a hobby of being one. He was a private, and I was a captain, and he insisted on that gulf being maintained.

Whenever he bade me good-night, after he had laid me in my bed and made me some cocoa — generally from his own supplies, for my parcels went astray — I could always hear him click his heels, and I knew he had saluted.

The second day after I had arrived at Osnabruck, he took me for exercise up and down the yard outside the canteen. This was my first appearance, and I was evidently an object of some curiosity, for wind had got round the camp that a blind prisoner had been brought in.

As the French officers passed me, I used to hear them say: "Good morning, Capitaine," or "Bon jour, mon camarade."

The English officers were splendid and always anxious to help me, and many a welcome supper of cocoa and cake I used to have in their rooms before going to bed.

I am afraid, though, that I used to make rather a big meal of it, as for the first two weeks I had to exist on the German rations.

When I took my first walk in the yard the canteen manager, his wife, and daughter were evidently watching out for me; for by and by, as a sign of their good-will, the daughter came running out after me with a present. It was an egg!

Cotton and I had a serious talk about this egg. He thought I should save it, and have half for supper and half for breakfast; but I settled the matter by eating it at once.

I think I have forgotten to mention that we were allowed to buy for half a mark, a loaf of bread every five days. I had no idea how far a loaf would go; I had never before given it a thought.

But Cotton had it down to a science; and worked it out that two small slices for breakfast, and the same for supper would carry me through, and he kept me to it.

"Cotton," I would say, after I had breakfasted on the two slices, "I could eat another slice."

"Better not, sir."

"Why not, Cotton? It's my loaf."

"This is the fourth day, sir, and if you have another slice, there will only be a small piece of crust for tomorrow's breakfast."

"All right, Cotton, I will sleep to dinner-time instead."

It was a joyful day when my first parcels arrived in camp. I was too excited about it to eat alone that day; and I invited young Martell of the R. N. A. S. to come and dine with me in my room.

There was a tin of soup and a tin of tripe and onions, and some biscuits and cheese. What a banquet! Martell and I decided to do ourselves in style. We even went so far as to send Cotton to the canteen for two glasses of what we indulgently patronised the canteen manager's humour by calling port wine.

Martell cooked the tripe and onions, after opening the tin with his penknife, and boiled it on the stove. The more we thought of that meal, the more we schemed to make a spread of it.

Cotton, too, rose to the occasion. From the canteen he obtained a sheet of white paper for a table-cloth, and by the side of each plate he placed a clean white handkerchief for serviettes.

The table was just a little rough, wooden one, about two feet square. The room was swept and the beds made to give the room a tidy appearance, and then we sat down.

Yes, Cotton understood. He knew that that meal was taking our thoughts back to England. It was taking him back, too. He knew that we imagined we were back again in the mess; and he imagined the same thing himself.

In that little room, and in the presence of that tin of tripe and onions we forget we were prisoners; we forgot that rows and rows of barbed wire bound us in captivity; we ignored the footsteps of the sentry pacing up and down outside our window, and the sharp yelping of the dogs.

We were back in the mess, and we chatted and laughed during the meal as we had done in the old days, while our spirits rose with the aroma of the tripe and onion; and Cotton stood behind me silent and attentive, removing the plates, washing them, and replacing them ready for the next course, pretending he was drawing plates from a well-filled pantry.

We finished our repast with biscuits and cheese, and then we solemnly stood, and raising our glasses, toasted the King.

Then we drew our chairs round the fire, and heating the coffee which was left over from breakfast, we bathed our thoughts in the aroma of two cigars which Cotton had thoughtfully provided for the occasion from the canteen.

Yes, people of England, living at home in luxury, by the protection of a thin line of khaki; when you become anxious at the prospect of one meatless day per week, try living for a fortnight on slops, and then appreciate the glories of a tin of tripe and onions.

Still, one can live on slops, and improve a meal by a vivid imagination. In fact, imagination is a distinct advantage when sitting down hungrily to a plate of thin watery soup and sloppy potatoes for dinner.

When the door used to open and Cotton appeared with this unsavoury repast, which was always the same each day, I would say to him in the most indifferent tone I could assume:

"Well, Cotton, what kind of soup is it to-day?"

"Well, sir; I really don't know. It might be anything; it looks like hot water."

"Why, my dear Cotton, this soup is salt. How dull you are! There must have been a battle in the North Sea!"

"How do you know that, sir?"

"It's the way the Germans have. This soup is hot seawater; it is to celebrate a victory."

The next day there would be a slight difference in the soup, and again Cotton would gravely shake his head, unable to fathom its mystery.

"My dear Cotton, when will you learn to gather information from your rations by a method of deduction?"

"Has there been another battle in the North Sea, sir?"

"No, my dear Cotton, the soup is thicker; the German fleet is back in the Kiel Canal."

It was the beginning of the third week of my sojourn in Osnabruck, when I was told one day that I was to proceed next morning to Blenhorst camp to appear before the Swiss Commission. Three other officers were also to go, including Rogan.

Cotton was to accompany me, and we made great preparation for the journey, packing in a tin box biscuits and cheese, chocolate and sardines; for although an officer is charged just the same for his full day's ration, the Germans have a habit of sending him on a long day's journey without food.

We started off at about 6 o'clock the next morning in high glee; for whatever the result of the Swiss Commission might be, there was the journey to Blenhorst to break the monotony of Osnabruck.

We had to change trains several times, and in the station restaurants we had much the same experience as I have described on my journey from Hanover.

In one restaurant we could only obtain a slice 223 of ham as thin as tissue-paper, and in another a very small sausage; and yet the German people we passed in the streets had no appearance of being short of food, or suffering any hardships in this respect. The people in the streets,

I understand, looked just as contented and well fed as the people in England.

The station for Blenhorst is about eight miles from the camp. A large flat, open lorry was sent to meet us to carry our baggage, but as our belongings were for the most part carried in our pockets, it was unnecessary for that purpose.

It then dawned upon our two guards, who had no more desire to walk than we had, that we might ride on the lorry ourselves. They obtained a form to hold four, and we four officers occupied this seat on the open lorry, Cotton sitting on the floor, while the two guards sat together behind us, with their feet dangling over the side.

That ride I shall never forget. Perhaps it was because I was blind that the situation seemed so ridiculously funny. The single-horsed lorry was pulled slowly through the rough, cobbled streets in sudden jerks, which sent our legs flying in the air, giving the form a tilt; and I expected every minute that we would all four turn a double somersault over the heads of our guards behind, and fall into the road like clowns at a circus.

Imagine the picture, an open lorry on a bitterly cold day going through the streets of a small German town with four British officers in uniform; two with their heads bandaged, another with an arm in a sling, and a fourth with a lame leg, all sitting on a form, shivering with cold — all smoking cigars; while people came out and gazed in open-mouthed wonder at the strange spectacle; and a crowd of little urchins came running behind, yelling at the top of their voices.

All this was explained to me; and I imagined a great deal more, for the ridiculous situation could only be complete if a shower of rotten eggs were hurled at us as we passed by.

The following morning the Swiss Commission arrived, and all those who wished to appear before it were ordered to assemble in the yard.

It was a pathetic assembly, officers and men maimed and afflicted beyond repair, waited in a long queue for their turn to go in and hear their fate.

There were a number of Tommies acting as orderlies in the camp who had been prisoners since Mons. There was nothing physically the matter with them; yet the silent and hopeful manner in which they took their position in the line, knowing as they must have done, that their chances were hopeless, was most pitiful to witness.

Yet, the same men, on appearing before the Commission, and being immediately rejected, laughed and joked as they returned to their work.

The British Tommy is heroic, and rough though his language sometimes is, he is a man, and Britain is his debtor.

CHAPTER XXXI

FREE

I BLUFF THE GERMAN SERGEANT
AACHEN
TWO BOTTLES OF WINE
ACROSS THE FRONTIER
GREAT SCOTT! I AM CHARGED FOR MY OWN
DEATH EXPENSES

I WAS PASSED for England!

The Examination Board consisted of a Swiss doctor, a German doctor, and the camp commandant. The Swiss doctor was provided with a schedule of disablements under which prisoners could be passed for exchange to their own country, and partial disablements for Switzerland, and frequently objections to a prisoner's application would be made by the German representative.

Of our party from Osnabruck, one was rejected, two were passed for Switzerland, and I was passed for England.

The decision of the Swiss Commission is not final, for, on being sent to the border, all prisoners are again examined — this time by German doctors only — and by their decision prisoners are frequently rejected and sent back to camp.

The final examination for those going to Switzerland takes place at Konstanz, and for those going to England, at Aachen.

I knew of one British Tommy who, during eighteen months had been twice passed for England and once for Switzerland, and each time rejected at the border, and he is to-day still in Germany.

It was about two weeks after I had been passed by the Swiss Commission that a German non-commissioned officer came to my room, and told me that I was to leave at 4 A.M. the next morning for England.

I had waited for this moment for three long months; I had no occupation of any kind, and spent most of my time lying on my bed or sitting on an uncomfortable chair before the fire, in hourly expectation of the door opening to tell me of my freedom.

Permission had been granted me to take Cotton with me to the border, so we packed all the food we had in stock and prepared for the journey. After travelling for some hours, we arrived at Hameln camp, where we were to stay the night. There was no accommodation for officers in the camp, and they apparently did not know what to do with me, or how to provide me with food, as they had never been called upon before to take charge of an officer.

The only spare hut was some distance down the road, but as this was outside the camp, a special guard had to be mounted outside my door. The question of feeding me was evidently found to be rather a perplexing one, and a German N. C. O., who could speak English, came to see me about it.

"You do not get the same rations at Osnabruck as private soldiers? No?"

I saw an opportunity and took it.

"No, special food is always provided for officers."

"What do you usually get?"

"Meat, vegetables, pudding or fruit, and coffee."

"Zo! But how much do you get? Do you get *all* that?"

"Yes. As much as we like to pay for."

"But the money. How do you pay?"

"Oh, I will pay cash before I leave."

"Goot. I will send you a dinner."

"By the way, what about my orderly? Bring in the same for him."

"Is dot usual? I vill gif him rations mit der men."

"That's against regulations in Osnabruck. Officers pay for their orderlies' food. Bring him the same as me. By the way, sausages and coffee for breakfast for both."

The meals were excellent, and I was glad we were moved off next day before the commandant came back to discover that I had bluffed the sergeant.

At the end of the following day we arrived in Aachen, and again, being the only officer, the difficulty arose about my accommodation.

This time I was placed in a real hospital which was used for German officers, and the accommodation was quite as good as I would expect in England. There were six nurses in this hospital, kind and generous in their treatment, and they fed me with every delicacy they could find, and waited upon me hand and foot.

Cotton was ordered to return to Osnabruck, and was replaced by a German orderly. An armed guard was placed outside my bedroom door, day and night, and whenever I took exercise in the garden, I could hear his footsteps behind me, following me wherever I went, and spitting on the ground every two or three yards.

On the second day after my arrival, I went for my final examination, and the medical officer told me he would send his sergeant-major, who could speak good English, to have a talk with me that evening. What did that mean? Why should he want to talk to me? I became suspicious and awaited his coming with some uneasiness.

He arrived about 7 o'clock that evening, bringing a friend and two bottles of wine. They opened the wine and we smoked together. Conversation was going to be very difficult. I felt I was going to be pumped for information.

It was going to be a battle of wits — I could feel it in my veins.

I made up my mind to be pleasant and tactful and meet every question by asking one.

As a matter of fact, I was mistaken. They were Germans who had lived in England and worked at the Deutsche Bank in George Yard, Lombard Street, until war broke out, and had lived in Highbury. I soon found out that they were not bad fellows at all, although their opening conversation did put my back up, and make me suspicious.

"London must be full of soldiers?"

I replied cautiously: "Well, I suppose the big cities, London, Paris, Berlin, Vienna, must all be full of soldiers these days."

"But what do the English people really think about the cause of the war?"

"Well," I replied evasively, "it's difficult to say, because people in England who talk, don't think; and people who think, don't talk."

"Well, do you think when the war is over there will be any hard feeling? Do you think things will settle down, and we shall be able to live there again as we did before?"

"Well, that depends upon the people's feelings after the war."

"You know, we cannot understand the English people; you are very hard to understand, the way you do things."

"How so?"

"Well, look at the way you have got your army together. It's marvellous; we all admit it. It surprised us."

"Look at your colonies. We thought Canada and Australia would break away; or at the very best, would not send over more than about 50,000 men."

"But what we cannot understand is why a country which can organise and handle such an enormous army, is unable to manage its civilian population."

"In what way do you mean?"

"Well, look at Ireland; fancy allowing that sort of thing! And the strikes you have! You build an army, and then allow your people to hinder it by striking."

"How can you help it?"

"You don't find strikes in Germany, because we organise our civil population for war, as well as the military population.

"There was one strike a little while ago, not for more money, but because the men felt they were not getting the food they were entitled to. Do you know what we did? — We put them all in uniform, and sent them on to the Somme, and we sent back from the Somme an equal number of soldiers to replace them in the factory."

"When do you think the war will be over?" I asked.

"When each side realises that it can't exterminate the other. Look what we've done on the Somme! You've lost, let us say, 700,000 men, and we have lost, say 500,000; and how far have you got? You'll never beat us. If you bend us back more, all we shall have to do is to retire to a new line, and you will have to begin your work all over again. You can bend, but you can't break us."

"Well, you tried it, and now it's our turn."

"Yes; but it will never end that way. Do you know that for months past we've been digging a new line, a straight line between Lille and Verdun, which will shorten our line by half? And if you bend that we will build another farther back. It can go on for ever at that rate."

"What about the blockade?"

"Of course, that's a farce. You've been doing your best to starve us for over two years. Do I look starved? We may not get as good food as we should like, but we get enough to live on, because we've got it properly systemised; whereas you let your people eat what they like."

Yes, there was truth in that; and after drinking all his wine, I turned into bed; for to-morrow I was to be free!

At 7 o'clock on the following evening motorcars, each with two trailers, went towards the station, filled with totally disabled soldiers, en route for England.

Even their captors thought it was not worth while to keep them.

War is a monstrous machine of the devil. At one end the manhood of Britain was pouring into its fiery cauldron; and here at the other end the devil was raking out the cinders.

My story is drawing to a close.

The hospital-train, bearing its human freight, passed through Namur, Liége, Brussels, and Antwerp to the Dutch frontier.

All who could do so looked eagerly out of the window for the moment when they would pass into freedom.

The train stopped at a small station right on the frontier, and some formalities were gone through. It started again — there was a German sentry — there was a Dutch sentry — we were over. Hurrah!!!

Cheer after cheer rang out from that long line of prostrate men.

The train pulled up at a little station just across the border. The door of my carriage was flung open and a number of Dutch girls came to my bed, and a shower of things came tumbling all about me as they passed one after the other, saying:

147

"Cigarettes, pleeze; apple, pleeze; cigar, pleeze; cake, pleeze; sweets, pleeze —"

I was in heaven.

My story is told.

I am back in my own home now; and as I conclude this record the postman brings me a letter. It is from my solicitors; I have torn it open, and find an account. The irony of fate closes the chapter:

"To services rendered in connection with the death of Captain Nobbs!"